GIMME
THE BALL

My Take On The Beautiful Game

Terry Curran

First Edition.
First published 2021

Published by:
Morgan Lawrence Publishing Services Limited
71-75 Shelton Street
Covent Garden
London
WC2H 9JQ
www.morganlawrence.co.uk
email: info@morganlawrence.co.uk
Company number: 12910264

ISBN: 9781838232924

A CIP catalogue record is available from the British Library.

Photographs are courtesy of: Sheffield Wednesday FC, Steve Ellis, Everton FC, Darren Griffiths, Derby County FC, Andy Ellis, Southampton FC, Duncan Holley.

Cover design by LCGraphix

Typesetting by Mathew Mann
Proofreading by Lois Hide

Printed and bound in Bulgaria
by Pulsio Print.

Contents

Foreword by Ron Atkinson
Former Sheffield Wednesday Manager

I FIRST came across Terry Curran when managing Cambridge United and he was a teenager with Doncaster Rovers.

He was part of a very good forward line with Brendan O'Callaghan, Peter Kitchen and Mickey Elwiss and we got absolutely battered. Goodness knows how we kept the score at 0-0 and then, after Donny finally scored towards the end, we equalised within 30 seconds. That was about the only time we went over the halfway line. I also remember he had a brilliant game for Derby against my West Brom in the FA Cup although we won the tie 3-2.

I had some great wide players at my clubs - Willie Johnston and Laurie Cunningham at West Brom, Steve Coppell and Gordon Strachan at United and Tony Daly at Villa – and I liked Terry Curran because he was a winger, who took on defenders and got at them. I never signed him, but he was a player who crossed my mind and I kept tabs on.

Terry is well loved at Sheffield Wednesday and it was there that I had my happiest days in management. He praises fellow Owls fans and I found out for certain how brilliant they are on the day we got relegated. That was a big personal disappointment. It all went to the last game of the season when we set a record for going down with 43 points. We had a supporters' club do that same night where we were clapped and cheered. I told the lads we owed these people big time.

I drove past the Aston Villa training ground on the way to Sheffield and was offered the job several times. They wanted me to replace Graham Taylor when he took the England job, but I refused it because I couldn't let Wednesday down.

We had a great time the following season when we got promoted and won the League Cup beating United at Wembley.

I made about six signings and not one of them disappointed. Roland Nilsson was the best right back I managed, Phil King was very good and John Sheridan one of the best midfield players of his generation. Carlton Palmer, whom I signed three times, was very underrated, Dalian Atkinson came from Ipswich and was sold for a lot of money and in Dave Hirst we had a top centre forward and as good and funny a lad as I have met.

Leaving Wednesday was the hardest decision of my managerial career. It was important to me though that I left them in good shape. I brought in Trevor Francis as a player after his sacking as player manager at QPR and recommended him to the board as my successor. I knew, if he could keep them sweet and fit, he had a very good squad to work with. It didn't surprise me they finished third in the First Division and reached two more cup finals.

When things started to go wrong again, Owls Chairman Dave Richards virtually pleaded with me to go back. Again, I signed a few players, including Emerson Thome, Andy Hinchcliffe and Niclas Alexandersson, and we picked up. In my first game we beat Arsenal on their way to the double, then toppled Manchester United and drew with Liverpool. We finished well clear of relegation and I genuinely thought that we could challenge for a European place the following season.

Dave Richards offered a three-year contract on reduced terms and wanted me to bring in someone to groom as a future manager. I selected Nigel Pearson who was all set to move from Carlisle to Sheffield to work with me. I also had Carlton Palmer and a striker lined up before I got tipped off that I might not be staying.

I told Richards I was off to Barbados and he needed to sort it out – and he never contacted me again. I bumped into him three years later when he was on England duty and had a pop at him about what happened.

You'll read in this book Terry's view on what has happened since. It's a shame for their loyal supporters because they are a great club who should be in the Premier League.

Introduction by Gabbie Cabbie
Podcaster and Poet

AS a general football fanatic, I loved 'mavericks' like Terry Curran, Alan Hudson, Rodney Marsh and Frank Worthington.

They were the ones who inspired me to try to emulate what they did on the pitch when I played football at a much lower level.

In recent years I've discovered more about them. I read and loved TC's first book *Regrets of a Football Maverick* and since then I've met both TC and Huddy, to name just two, through my podcasts.

Both *The Curran View* and *My Life My Music* with Alan Hudson have become very popular regular podcasts enjoyed by four-figure audiences.

I've found TC mirrors what I saw in him as a footballer. He didn't give a 'shit' who he was playing against, he went out onto that pitch and showed his talent. As a person, he has the same integrity and honesty. I've also found out he will do anything for anyone.

As I'm writing this, we've been working together for more than 18 months and produced 76 weekly episodes. Our fun chats include news and views on Sheffield Wednesday, book corner, topics from the week's football, our forecasts and choice of music.

The way TC played he said 'gimme me the ball' and backed himself. He took responsibility on the pitch and he does the same with his views on football and life. That's why I am excited that this is the title of his second book because, I know, it will be just as difficult to put down as his first.

You are very welcome to access any of my regular podcasts, also including *A Chapter of My Life* about football books and authors and *Game of My Life* featuring more football heroes worth remembering, by going onto Facebook and searching for SRB Media.

But, first, enjoy TC's latest work on football past and present . . .

PART ONE
MY FOOTBALL FAVOURITES

CHAPTER ONE
Me and Big Jack

By MICK PICKERING, Former SOUTHAMPTON and SHEFFIELD WEDNESDAY defender

TERRY CURRAN breezed into the dressing room at both Saints and Owls like a whirlwind and was a breath of fresh air.

We came to Southampton from different routes. I was in the Fourth Division with Barnsley whilst Terry was already a Division One regular with Derby. Lawrie McMenemy added experienced players like Chris Nicholl and Phil Boyer to his team after winning the FA Cup and then promotion.

Terry was quite confident and part of a group of four or five of us who socialised a lot with Alan Ball. We enjoyed good times watching horse racing and going out in London and also in Bournemouth where Ted MacDougall lived.

I lost my place after Lew Chatterley joined the club as McMenemy's right hand man. Jack Charlton had taken over as manager at Sheffield Wednesday and called Lawrie wanting an experienced centre half. That's how my move to Hillsborough came about.

As soon as I met Jack, I signed straightaway. Wednesday was nearer home and a good move for me as the manager made me club captain.

Again, Terry joined the club a little while later and made his presence felt. Terry always said what he wanted and how he thought the game should be played, whereas most of the other lads kept their feelings to themselves. There were a few cliques in that dressing room, involving the older and the younger players, but Terry wasn't part of that.

Terry did a great job for Wednesday when we needed it most. To be honest, he was almost unstoppable and formed a very good partnership up front with Andy McCulloch. Terry scored 20-odd goals and Andy wasn't far behind when we got promotion. Terry scored different kinds of goals. Pace is everything in the game and opponents couldn't cope with him.

We went on a long unbeaten run after the Boxing Day massacre of Sheffield United who were top of the league at the time. We got results at difficult places like Oxford, Swindon and Reading and always had a terrific following from Sheffield. The fans, including friends in my social circle, loved Terry to death.

Big Jack also did a great job. He had his quirks, but never held a grudge and was a lovely guy. I remember him coming up with an idea for me as a centre half. He told me that when I fouled someone to make a point of picking him up, dust him down and say sorry. I was doing that one afternoon at Luton when they took the free kick quickly and scored. Afterwards Jack told me to forget that advice!

I spent a lot of time socialising with Terry who had a house off Ecclesall Road, Sheffield. He was always good fun and very handy to be with as a single man because the women loved him.

Terry and Big Jack didn't always get on well but had respect for each other's abilities. I was the guy who got between them during the fight in the gymnasium and took Terry back to the dressing room. That was my duty as captain whilst Mel Sterland wanted the fight to continue because he was enjoying it!

Terry left Hillsborough before me and went to Sheffield United. That was pure Terry – the kind of thing he did. To be fair, he was one of a few players who went from Wednesday to United and vice versa. Like Terry, I'm very sad we've now lost Big Jack. The last time I saw him was at one of our Boxing Day reunions 25 years on in 2004. We went out for a meal on the Friday, watched a Wednesday game then had a function at Hillsborough.

I heard Jack gave up after dinner speaking because one night he forgot what he was going to say. What will never be forgotten though are all the memories, many of which are in Terry's book.

You'll enjoy looking back and also reading TC's views on Wednesday and modern day football.

*****

WE LAUGHED and fought, but I loved Big Jack.

It was a sad, sad day for me in July 2020 when I heard my former Wednesday boss and friend Jack Charlton had passed away. What a fantastic man he was! We never saw eye-to-eye on the way football should be played, but we always had a mutual love and respect because we were both winners.

He played a big part in my life because Big Jack had the guts to approach me when I was with Saints in the First Division to ask me to play for Wednesday who were struggling in the Third. The move made no sense for my career, but Jack knew I was a big Owls fan and saw Sheffield Wednesday as a sleeping giant who should be up there with the top clubs in the land.

Jack Charlton was already one of my heroes as a key member of England's 1966 World Cup winning team. Watching England beat West Germany 4-2 at Wembley to become world champions was one of the highlights of my childhood. I loved football and dreamt of being a professional, playing at Wembley and for England. I never thought that 13 years later I would be big mates with Alan Ball, one of the stars of 1966, and about to be signed by Jack Charlton.

I enjoyed watching Don Revie's great Leeds United side with Big Jack playing alongside Norman Hunter in central defence. I'm not a Leeds fan, but I admired Revie's style of keeping the ball and tiring out the opposition even on terrible pitches that they played on.

I know now that Big Jack had the same arguments with those Leeds players as we did at Wednesday. Leeds had great midfield players in Billy Bremner and Johnny Giles, yet Jack tried to keep them as far away as possible so he could launch the ball forward.

I met Big Jack for the first time in the Cinderella Rockefella night club after playing for Southampton against Leeds in the first leg of the League Cup semi final in 1979. I can tell you now my transfer from Saints to Wednesday was already well under way.

First contact came from Maurice Setters, my former manager at Doncaster Rovers and Big Jack's assistant at Hillsborough. Sadly, of course, Maurice himself passed away in November to add to a very sad 2020. He said that Big Jack wanted me at Wednesday and thought that, because I was an Owls fan, they would be able to persuade me. Yes, I was interested in joining them, I told him.

Setters called again a couple of days later to say that the boss was keen to speak with me in person. So Jack and I had our first contact on the phone and I was impressed with what I heard.

He said, although Wednesday were in the Third Division, they were a huge football club and this was a big project. "If we can get this right and take Wednesday back into the First Division, we'll get the freedom of Sheffield," he told me. "Don't worry about promotion, Jack, I'll do that for you," I said.

Jack was pleased that I was so confident and positive and I knew he was committed to helping the club that I loved. That meeting in the night club was arranged in a phone call a week before we played at Elland Road. Jack said that he and Maurice would be at the game and we should meet up in the night club later to talk further. Jack was at home in the pubs and clubs and a manager who socialised with the players. He was a good listener who took on board your opinion, yet always remained the boss.

Jack knew we were staying over in Leeds before travelling to Blackpool to play Preston North End three days later in the FA Cup, so it was a good plan. I gave him good value on the field on that icy night as Saints fought back from two goals down to somehow get away with a 2-2 draw after Leeds battered us.

Alan Ball, always up for a good night out, had no idea what he was walking into. "Your mate Big Jack is going to be here," I said.

"How do you know that?" he asked.

I told him Jack wanted to take me to Wednesday and Bally wasn't happy.

Bally bought four tequila sunrises and said to Jack "Here's to great memories; to all the lads who won the World Cup." All four of us toasted England's greatest achievement.

The chat flowed between Bally, the dynamic ball playing midfielder, and Big Jack, the no-nonsense centre back. I only wish that all my mates from Kinsley, my home village, could have been there to see me with two of my heroes. Bally told Jack: "You won't be signing him; Terry is too good for the Third Division." Jack replied that he would be signing me, but there were no ill feelings between them - it was all good football banter. When their talk ended, Big Jack asked if I still wanted to sign for Wednesday. I said yes but wanted to see if we beat Leeds in the second leg so I could play at Wembley.

A few weeks later I scored the winning goal for Saints - not such good news for Jack. "That's blown it now," he said. "I wanted to bed you into the club before the end of the season, so we could give you a good pre-season ready for a promotion push."

I told him: "Don't worry, I'll be there and my fitness will be fine."

Jack had to be seen to be doing things by the book with Saints manager Lawrie McMenemy. He then phoned to say that McMenemy 'wasn't playing ball' and that I should ask for a move.

Once the League Cup final was over, things moved quickly and my mind was made up. McMenemy removed any last doubt by leaving me out of the FA Cup quarter final replay against Arsenal at Highbury, much to Bally's disgust. He had no idea why but said McMenemy wanted me to meet former Derby County winger Alan Hinton, now the manager of Seattle Sounders. He wanted to take me to the MLS in a deal that McMenemy had arranged. Hinton said he liked me from my days at Forest and would have swapped notes no doubt with Brian Clough. The £11,000 signing on fee was good, but the move was wrong. I told Hinton I was 23 years old, beginning to play well in the First Division and had a future in England with Sheffield Wednesday.

I went into McMenemy's office every day to ask for a transfer. He did his best to keep me and there was a new three-year contract on the table. Instead I spent the next three years at Wednesday, which included our promised promotion from the Third Division in the season when I starred in the Boxing Day massacre and won the division's Golden Boot, and in the next two seasons when we looked on course to get into the First Division until fading towards the end.

We both saw football the way we played it. Big Jack was a defender; I was a forward. Jack's first thought was how to stop us conceding goals, I wanted to score them. Jack went crazy after we conceded a very late equaliser in a derby match against Chesterfield at Hillsborough. Spireites reckoned that it was about 6pm when Geoff Salmons scored to deny us victory. I blamed the referee for adding on so much time, Jack blamed us for losing the ball.

So we spent much of the next week in practicing 'killing time'. They call it 'game management' nowadays. This involved me as

Jack knew that I was good at getting the ball into the corner and holding onto possession. I won't kid you – this was boring me to death. I was a top footballer, one of the most naturally talented in the game, I could run the ball into the corner in my sleep. Andy McCulloch saw it was winding me up and Big Jack knew it too. Yet he hammered the same point, so I would do as I was told.

I told Andy what I planned to do if we were beating Rotherham with a few minutes to go at Hillsborough on the Saturday - run the ball into the corner, turn back, run the full length of the pitch and pass it back to our goalkeeper Bob Bolder! That would kill time and flip Big Jack's lid.

Andy dared me to do it, knowing I had the balls. Many Sheffield Wednesday fans remember what happened next. We were winning 5-0 and there was no chance of Rotherham getting back into the game when I got the ball 10 yards into their half. I ran full pelt back into the corner at the Leppings Lane, then turned back and sprinted almost the full length of Hillsborough to pass the ball back to Bolder. Some of the crowd laughed, others booed and Big Jack went crazy. You would have thought we had lost 5-0.

But, as former Leeds teammate Alan Clarke rightly pointed out in his tribute to Jack, he was never off with anyone for long. He asked if we were going to The Travellers in Hillsborough as usual. As I was getting out of the car, Jack shouted: "Get me a pint of Guinness, TC". That was me and Big Jack and that's why I loved him.

On the training pitch, Jack practiced corners, free kicks and other dead ball situations for a good 45 minutes. Jack talked about the opposition for a good two hours, from knowing the importance of not having the ball to how dangerous our opponents could be if we lost concentration.

We also looked at what to do in possession, spending hours on certain patterns of play. Jack did all the coaching and demanded we did what he said or we got a right bollocking. Fans watched us train at Middlewood Road, so some of you will remember those days.

Talking with the great Billy Bremner in the boot room and in pubs, he said my arguments with Big Jack reminded him of how Jack clashed with his manager Don Revie over his football philosophy. Billy told me 'Jack does love you, you know' but I reminded him of how he argued with Revie. Jack had learnt his lesson from falling out with fellow Leeds players and, if I sat down with him and talked, we wouldn't argue so much, Billy said.

The problem was I knew how football should be played and couldn't go back on that. A couple of years playing for Cloughie at Forest was a big part of my football education. Clough showed how a passing game with a tempo could succeed in a country where most teams played the long ball into channels and tried to win it back. Forty years later we're beginning to learn he was right!

Clough's way suited me as a skilful player and still very quick, despite the injury which I suffered at Forest. Had I been given the freedom to express myself and float across the front line, I would have scored more goals than I did at Hillsborough. I thought that the midfield players in our Second Division side could have been used to give me and the other strikers better service. But Jack said he didn't have the players to play that way and wanted to keep the ball as far away from our goal as possible.

It came down to this. I never wanted to play the football we played at Wednesday, but I did so out of respect for the manager and the club. Jack mostly wanted me to play wide. I preferred to roam along the front line. I hated being stuck out on the flank with the ball flying over my head and then spending so much time chasing back to win back possession gifted to the opposition. That eventually led us to fight in the gymnasium – the proper story of which is coming soon! The Wednesday lads laughed at us as if we were a married couple always at each other's throats, but mates to the last.

People ask who was the toughest manager that I ever played for and I answer Big Jack without any doubt. But he was also the guy you wanted to go to war with. He had the personality to win you over because he was straight and down-to-earth.

Jack had his own unique way of showing me that he was on my side whilst playing by the rules. He didn't like his players getting booked for dissent which happened to me a lot for lashing out verbally after defenders tried to kick me off the pitch. Jack told me that would cost me £100 in front of all the players after the match. On Monday morning, Maurice Setters said Jack wanted to see me in his office. The boss asked when I was going to learn not to get booked and I replied 'the day they stop fouling me'. Jack said he was fining me £100 and I said I wasn't going to pay for being kicked from pillar to post. Jack had a float in the safe in his office which must have been the club's money. He then took out £100, handed it to me and I handed it back to him! Afterwards he told the press I'd been fined for dissent.

Jack was the boss and never gave in. He didn't want to lose at football or anything else in life. We even argued over snooker and table tennis. I beat him at both, so he made up his own rules. Alan Biggs, a reporter for Radio Hallam, was waiting to interview Jack as we were playing snooker at the ground. Jack played a shot which I called out as a foul and then went on one of his rants. Jack looked at Biggsy and said: "I'm right, aren't I, Alan?' Biggsy said he didn't know, but would ask someone in the snooker world. . Jack had a £5 bet on the game with 'this little twat' and refused to pay up until he heard from Biggsy about the foul shot. Biggsy made a statement live on the radio that Terry Curran was right about the foul shot and Big Jack was wrong, When Biggsy got back in touch, Jack went crazy and was lost for words for a few moments. Then Jack said: 'let's get on with the interview' and it was all forgiven and forgotten. That was Big Jack all over.

Our other joint sporting interest was the dogs. We co-owned a greyhound with Andy McCulloch. My interest was from my Kinsley days and there was a local racetrack at Owlerton. Jack's Irish contact led us to a dog called Spiral Please and all three of us chipped in £600 to buy him. That looked good when he won his first race, but it didn't last.

Spiral Please was due to race again on the Saturday when Wednesday had an important game. But I got a phone call a few days before to tell me that our dog had suffered an injury. So I picked him up from trainer Harry Crapper to go to Hillsborough for infrared treatment. I knew I was on safe ground because Big Jack co-owned the dog even when I saw Mel Sterland, one of the younger Owls lads, on the treatment table. I told him to get off because it was far more important that the dog was fit than Mel! Luckily, he's a great lad and saw the funny side. In the end Mel was passed fit and Wednesday won, the dog ran and lost.

I played for 15 clubs because of my big mouth and my philosophy on how the game should be played. But never at any of those clubs did managers do the things that Big Jack did. If any of our fans got stranded at an away game, he gave them a free trip home. Typically, he said 'sit at the back, don't bother the lads' but soon invited them to join in. Great memories.

Jack Charlton was also a family man – I saw that with my own eyes. His wife Pat treated me like a son which is probably why I got so many bollockings. One day I was in a shop called Scoles in the centre of Sheffield having coffee with a young woman, who wasn't my wife, when we saw Jack and Pat, who looked a little embarrassed. Next morning Jack pulled me to one side and warned: "When you are doing something like that, always make sure you're not local!" I met a different woman in the same café next day and who walked in but Jack and Pat! That earned me another grilling from the boss.

Jack and Pat's lovely home was open house for all Wednesday players. I went there about five or six times whilst at Hillsborough and was always made to feel welcome. Jack and his wife were good listeners, coming from a working class background. He told the lads to 'give me a cig, kid' and was happy talking football with anyone. He was a very, very sociable guy. Big Jack liked footballers, often inviting them to go shooting and fishing with him – neither of which were my thing.

Jack had a pool table that he liked to play on whilst Pat is one of the nicest people you could ever meet. She was polite and open and I never saw her sulk or be angry. I met Jack's mum a couple of times and she reminded me of Pat.

They were a rock solid couple although I did have doubts for a couple of minutes. We were staying in a hotel on the Friday night ahead of a match at Southend. Never a good sleeper, I woke up at 6am and went downstairs for a newspaper. Back in my room, Tony Toms, the SAS man that Len Ashurst brought in as our trainer, knocked on the door. Tony made us laugh in the Owls dressing room but wasn't someone to cross. This time he really got me going. He said Big Jack had pulled a couple of birds and I should knock on his door to find out what was going on. I was greeted by Jack looking like Rob Nesbitt – hair all over the place, dressed in his y-fronts and a vest, rubbing his eyes to show that I'd woken him up.

"What the hell do you want?" he asked, as I scanned the room for non-existent women. I'd been well and truly done to get myself into trouble. Jack said I shouldn't be up at an unearthly hour when I needed to rest.

I said don't worry, we'll beat Southend no problem. We drew 0-0, but Jack was fine with me and saw the joke.

Most of us laugh at dark things and the Wednesday lads joked about Big Jack's memory. Even 40 years ago he got names wrong. Jack and Pat had new players stay at their house, including Andy McCulloch and Jeff King – he called them Jeff McCulloch and Andy King. We didn't think anything of it at the time.

He looked like a holidaymaker in his training kit and amused us by reading the scouting reports on our opponents. These were always handwritten by one of his staff sent to watch them the previous week. Jack tried to read them word for word to us on the day of the game before getting to a bit that he couldn't read because of the bad handwriting. Then he handed the note over to Maurice Setters who could never read it either.

The team was posted on the noticeboard and Jack copied it down on the back of a cigarette packet with one or two tactical notes. But in the dressing room he was always very clear. Defenders shouldn't take chances; midfielders were warned against 'tippy tappy football' with the ball played long 'so TC can chase it'. We were in good books if we carried out his orders to the letter and got bollocked if we didn't.

Like many managers, Big Jack tried to come up with big ideas to make a difference – something nobody had thought of. It happened after I fluffed a couple of free kicks in a match against Newcastle at St James' Park. I scored a couple that season but smashed these high over the bar. Jack went mad, saying I'd never take another free kick for him to which I said I wasn't bothered.

Later that week Jack revealed our new free kick move. This involved me and Gary Banister forming a two-man Owls wall in front of the opposition's wall. For some reason he wanted Gary Megson to take the kick. As he was about to shoot, the two of us were to walk back towards the ball bent over. Megson's shot should deflect off our backs and into the net! I couldn't stop myself laughing, so Big Jack ordered me off the training pitch. I was looking on when the manager decided to show us how to do it. He shambled up to the ball, looking like Mike Bassett with his tracksuit bottoms three quarters up and one football sock and one ordinary sock, and somehow it worked exactly as he said. The ball ended up in the back of the net. We couldn't believe it.

When we got a free kick within shooting distance, Megs did something more sensible then told Big Jack that he didn't 'think it was on, boss'. Likewise, Big Jack surprised us when he got frustrated at 'Spider' Mellor trying to take a corner in training. Twice he put the ball behind the goal, so Jack decided to do it himself and delivered the perfect ball!

During my last few months at Wednesday, I tried to reason with Big Jack about a new contract. We were struggling to agree terms when he invited me into his office for a chat. I asked for an £11,000 tax free signing on fee and £500 a week. Jack refused, claiming that I was already earning more at Wednesday than he was. I saw a £33,000 invoice on Jack's desk addressed to the club for improvements made to his house at Worsborough and doubted if that was the case.

So I suggested a different way of sorting out my deal that would have been good both for Wednesday and myself. I suggested that the club didn't pay me any wages but gave me permission to sort out my own personal sponsors and put their names on my shirt. I already had a personalised car from VW Guilders, of Sheffield, with repair bills, tax and insurance all included for three years – and was being asked by building societies to open new branches. Jack said that the club would never allow it and that there was no way this would happen in football. Nowadays, of course, shirt sponsorship is an everyday part of professional football.

The contract went unsigned with Jack willing to meet my terms, but not pay the tax. This left me free to talk with other clubs and chairman Reg Brealey made me a good financial offer to join Sheffield United. I'm sorry to admit that I wanted to rub Big Jack's nose in it by signing for The Blades. It also suited my social life to stay in Sheffield. A tribunal fixed the fee at £100,000. There and then Big Jack offered to pay the tax and forget about the proposed transfer, but it was too late. I had shaken on a deal with Brealey and wasn't going back on it.

I was sad that Jack never got Wednesday back where we belonged. But, without doubt, he turned the club round before Howard Wilkinson guided Owls into the First Division. If I had to compare him with a modern manager, I'd say David Moyes or Sam

Allardyce. Had Big Jack got us promoted, he was good enough to ensure that we wouldn't have been in any trouble without having the X-factor for us to challenge near the top.

Later in his managerial career, Jack took over at the Republic of Ireland and became a national hero all over again. Not many are heroes in two countries, but Big Jack gave the Irish memories to treasure. Jack's best remembered for taking Ireland to the last eight of the World Cup in 1990 – the furthest they ever got in any international competition – where they lost 1-0 by hosts Italy. But he did much more than that. They also got to the knockout stages of the 1994 World Cup in America, qualified for the Euros in 1988 and were close to doing so again in 1992.

Jack inherited very talented players, including Liam Brady, Frank Stapleton, David O'Leary, Kevin Sheedy and John Aldridge, but when you listen to the Irish lads, he succeeded exactly the same way as he did with Wednesday.

He got rid of 'tippy tappy' players and told his lads to hit the the ball long and harry the opposition's back four into mistakes. Reading between the lines, the Irish players didn't like his style, but liked him.

He pulled them together as a group by getting rid of the cliques of the 'superstar' players and ensuring that they enjoyed being on international duty.

Big Jack never did get the freedom of Sheffield, but the freedom of Dublin was no bad consolation. I never wanted to watch his team play but respected what they achieved.

We should have handled our differences better. Meeting him at a game between Everton and Leeds, the big man said he should have given me the tax money and avoided the transfer tribunal that led me to sign for Sheffield United. And, of course, I shouldn't have allowed my disagreements with him to influence the move.

In more recent years when we met for reunions at Hillsborough, the lads were more worried about Big Jack. We all knew that something was wrong and this was no longer a laughing matter. He was suffering from dementia which is one of the worst things in this life.

When I produced my first book *Regrets of a Football Maverick*, I wanted Big Jack to do the foreword – and he gladly agreed. My writer, John Brindley, told me the great man got almost all his memories wrong, but we put them right. His heart was still in the right place and he spoke fondly of me as I did of him.

I got a message about two weeks before his passing that he didn't have long to live, but it was still a shock when the news came through. My phone rang with requests for interviews as a former player associated with Big Jack but, out of respect, I didn't speak with anyone. It was too raw and I needed to take it in myself.

RIP Big Jack until we meet again. I loved you and I'll always be proud that someone of your stature in the game gave me the chance to play for Wednesday.

CHAPTER TWO
Simply The Best And The Top One

I DON'T do starstruck. I met many famous people through football and my busy social life and never bowed down to any. I only got a few autographs because they don't mean much to me.

But there were two people who I describe as special and whose autographs I did want. I idolised them when I was a teenage football fan and they were just as brilliant when I met them as a professional player.

George Best was the first superstar footballer in England; the first just as likely to be on the front as the back page of a newspaper.

I began watching him in the late 1960s when he burst onto the scene as an exciting forward at Manchester United. He was brilliant as United became the first English team to lift the European Cup with a 4-1 win over Benfica at Wembley in 1968 It's easy to forget in today's world of media hype how unique the Irishman was. Young people look at celebrities, music stars and others as role models. They dream about being like them. George Best, for many reasons, was the one I looked up to.

He was a fantastic one-off footballer. Go on YouTube and you'll find magical George Best moments. Never a negative thought in his head, he glided past opponents as if they weren't there. His skill and close control made good players look stupid and he had the ability and composure to finish. George Best was one of the few players who lit up the game. Whenever Manchester United or Northern Ireland were playing, George made the game interesting – all eyes were on him. It's the hardest skill in football to create, to unlock, to do something out of the ordinary. Most players work hard and do the basics, but very few can get fans out of their seats.

Nobody in England's famous 1966 World Cup team, fascinated

my young eyes as much as Best. In my opinion, Best was the greatest footballer ever. Johan Cruyff did the most good for the game as a player and a coach but George lived up to his name. He was right up there with Messi, Ronaldo, the Brazilian Ronaldo, Zidane, Zico, Rivellino, Pele and Maradona. Saying one was better than the others is just opinion.

Unlike the others on that list, George didn't play regularly with other superstars. Most played for teams who regularly won matches and trophies. You'll never see Cristiano Ronaldo and Lionel Messi in a bad football team. Pele and Rivellino played with one of the best teams I have seen in my life when Brazil won the 1970 World Cup in magical style. But George Best played in a Manchester United side that went from brilliant to average, plus a poor Northern Ireland.

Chatting with Best. I know the mediocrity of his teammates caused him to lose focus. He was probably making more money from his TV commercials and appearances than playing for Manchester United. Life was pretty good for him with girls and money, but I don't think he would have gone into early retirement had he been allowed to go to Chelsea.

It would have suited his lifestyle, too, for he was spending more time socialising in London than in Manchester. Bestie was trapped because United wouldn't let him go to one of their main rivals and left to suffer in a team whose other star players were past their best.

George was the reason I still like Manchester United. I watched him every time I could even though there was nothing like the amount of football on TV as there is now. One game I will always remember was in 1970. Fast forward to today and it would be a nothing game between Northampton Town and Manchester United in the FA Cup. Mud heap of a pitch, two mismatched sides, there would be merely a mild interest in whether Northampton could spring a shock.

But this game was special because George Best was back from suspension. And he transformed that tie into an unforgettable occasion. Scoring six goals in any match is incredible but Best did it with a variety of goals – a couple of headers, twice dummying his way round the goalkeeper and close-range finishes. I swear when I spoke with the Northampton goalkeeper Kim Book, who later played with me at Donny, he was still giddy from the way the great man sent him the wrong way to score the final goal.

When I began my professional career, I wanted to be like George Best, go past defenders, score goals and thrill the crowds. I wanted to be the next superstar. I knew how good I was, but never as good as my idol.

I never played on the same pitch as him. But having George Best compliment me for my ability and then spend time with me drinking and chatting were great privileges.

The nearest I got to him during his career was in the 1976/77 season after Best signed for Second Division Fulham. Forest went to Craven Cottage on the opening day, but unfortunately the great man was in the stands rather than playing. There was a lot of media interest about how much George had left in his tank after he had eventually quit Manchester United and retired before spending a short time playing in America. Even before kicking off I had one eye on George Best as I spotted him dressed down in a blue hoodie and jeans and still looking very fit. He was tanned and looked physically well.

I had plenty to prove at Forest after my first season had been hit by illness and desperately wanted to impress my idol. That moment came when I picked up the ball on the halfway line, waltzed past a couple of defenders and lobbed the ball into the top corner from about 35 yards. It was one of those perfect moments. The best goal of my entire football career, better even in my opinion than my goal at Bramall Lane. I put my arms up in the air and dedicated that perfect moment to Bestie.

After scoring twice to help Forest to a 2-2 draw, I had the privilege of meeting him in the players' lounge. Best came straight up to me and said: 'you can play football; you are some player'. I told him he was my favourite footballer of all time and he replied that he had enjoyed watching me play. Those were words I will always remember.

I went on to play some of the best football of my life in the next few months helping Forest to tear apart visitors to the City Ground until that serious injury against Burnley brought me crashing down to earth. I hated missing every match during that long layoff, but one of the biggest disappointments was still being a long way from fitness when Fulham visited Forest in January.

Best was in a Fulham side, including that other great entertainer Rodney Marsh and England's 1966 World Cup winning captain Bobby Moore. I was in the stand watching as even George Best couldn't stop Forest as we won 3-0. My big moment came afterwards when Ian 'Bomber' Bowyer sent me into the Fulham dressing room to get some autographs and Best's in particular. Again, we had a brief chat with Best asking me how I was getting on with my recovery and said: "I want to see you back playing football very soon."

Fast forward a couple of years and I had the pleasure of three much longer meet ups with George Best, thanks to our mutual pal Alan Ball. Bally told me on the Wembley pitch after Southampton had been beaten 3-2 by my old Forest side in the 1979 League Cup final that he was going out later to Tramps, the London night club.

There was always a host of big stars in Tramps, a Who's Who of actors, pop stars and other celebrities. That night we saw Oliver Tobias, Michael Caine and Olivia Newton John, but when George Best walked in everyone was looking at him.

The guy had incredible presence. The bluest of blue eyes, black hair, good looking, he literally lit up a room and people flocked to him. Everyone thought he belonged to them. Everyone wanted to be George Best's friend.

We sipped champagne and chatted about football. Bally asked George whether he would have quit the game as he did at United had he been allowed to go to Chelsea. That was the club for flair players who liked to live life to the full, both on and off the field. Bally suggested that George could have been the final piece in the jigsaw to push Chelsea's very talented side over the line to win more trophies. Best agreed but realised that was never going to happen.

Looking at him that night though he didn't seem to be missing out too much. What he had lost on the football pitch, he had gained through a glamorous lifestyle.

Bally also organised the other two drinking sessions that we had with George, both of which were also in London. He phoned me up to see if I wanted to go to Terry Venables' wine bar. Then he dropped his car off at my place and we went by taxi and train to the capital. For me, meeting up with George again was as exciting as playing in a cup final.

We were tucked away in a corner out of sight, but that didn't stop people from coming to see George. He was a shy man at heart who could never be left alone. People constantly came up to him, offering to buy him a drink or ask for an autograph and he could never say no. When out and about, his life was never his own and that wasn't easy to handle. Women were literally all over him. He didn't even have to chat them up, they'd be pressing their phone numbers into his hand. And I'm talking about very good-looking women.

Bestie started off with three or four glasses of wine, then followed up with vodka and Baileys and a Pernod and Black. He was fine for most of the evening, being used to holding his drink, but was quite tipsy by the time we left. Bally loved gin and tonic and joined in with the vodka and Baileys whilst I had wine. George wasn't suffering as he did later in life. He looked fit and more in control of things, although he sometimes missed training through drink. He was a good-looking guy who had amazing blue eyes that attracted women to him.

The last time we all got together was in a wine bar on Chelsea's Kings Road where we were joined by Peter Osgood. The chat was normal stuff – football, managers, gambling and women. We were just guys having a good time.

It made George chuckle – and me too – when he was asked about why it all went wrong. He had just won £17,000 in a casino in Leicester and was shagging Miss World, Mary Stavin. He played football at the highest level, winning virtually everything possible, apart from the World Cup, and met endless famous people. He lived life more in a year than most do in a lifetime.

We all know how sadly George's story ended when he passed away in 2005, aged just 59, a few years after having a liver transplant. Alcohol is a strange thing. It's never bothered me. I drunk much less than most footballers during my playing career and I don't drink that often now. George was different. He got addicted to alcohol and it played a big role in ruining, then ending, his life. He should have had my attitude towards drink, I wanted his unique ability as a footballer. Even now, he's still my hero because he was my kind of player and person.

We don't all get to meet our idols in this life and sometimes that's good. They don't always live up to our expectations because what we see on TV or in Hollywood isn't real life. But meeting and spending time with George Best was even better than I imagined. He had a magic that attracted people like a magnet but, at heart, he was like all of us – an ordinary guy. I just had a few opportunities to meet Bestie, but far more time to get to know my second idol, Brian Clough.

I first set eyes on him when, as a young football fan, I went with a few mates to Oakwell to watch Barnsley play Hartlepools. We stood at the side of the dugout where a young Clough was urging his team on.

I knew that he had been a footballer who had scored a stack full of goals for Middlesbrough and Sunderland before his career was ended at the age of 25 through a cruciate ligament injury. When you look up his record of 251 goals in 274 league games, it was incredible by any standards – and something he reminded us all about fairly often!

Back then he was just the away manager of a struggling Fourth Division team who caught my attention. He was very vocal and there was something about him – something about the way he was talking to his players that I liked.

My next sight of him was on TV as he inspired Derby County in the early 1970s. It was then that I realised he was both a great manager and a TV personality – and I liked him for both.

A film has been made in recent years titled *I believe in Miracles* giving some idea of how incredible his achievements were at Forest. But let's not forget that he performed miracles at the Baseball Ground as well.

Derby were in a lowly place in the Second Division when he took over. By the time he left they had been promoted, won a First Division title and reached the semi finals of the European Cup, where many felt they were beaten by the referee rather than Juventus.

That gave him the chance to become better known through interviews on sports and other TV programmes during which his unique personality came across. Like Best, Cloughie oozed confidence and charisma. When he said something, right or wrong, we listened. We all wanted more and more of a guy clearly different from the mainstream. I liked his arrogance and brashness.

Cloughie said it himself but it was the way he succeeded that was as impressive as all his trophies. Derby County and Nottingham Forest both played football and entertained fans. They had very, very good – and occasionally great players – but the teams were even better than the sum of all the players' talents. Both had great belief and confidence in their way of playing and the manager. And so much of that was down to Brian Clough.

My first connection with Clough as a player will surprise a few people. For, although he eventually signed me for Forest, it was during his famous 44 days at Leeds United that he made his first approach for me. I was in the early weeks of my second season at Donny when I took a phone call from Maurice Edwards who worked for Clough at several of his clubs. He sounded me out about a possible move to Elland Road. Of course, I would have jumped at the chance of playing for the First Division champions.

Unfortunately, things didn't go any further because Cloughie was out the door almost as quickly as he arrived. It's total speculation what would have happened to me had he stayed longer and followed up his interest. Clough took a lot of stick for his signings at Leeds as he tried to make up for the suspension of his captain Billy Bremner, who was sent off with Kevin Keegan in the Charity Shield at Wembley. John McGovern and John O'Hare were both experienced players but associated in the minds of Leeds supporters with a Derby side who they hated – partly because of the bad blood which Clough fuelled between the two clubs.

I regard McGovern as my mate – he was even best man at my wedding – but I can understand why the fans didn't rate him compared with Bremner and Johnny Giles who were world class midfield players.

So how would it have gone down if he had signed me from lowly Doncaster Rovers? I will never know, nor do I know whether Cloughie would have been a success at Elland Road had the board backed him. Taking on a club expected to be at the top of the league after what Don Revie had achieved was hard enough, never mind the fact that some of the players were coming towards the end of their careers and Clough made it even more difficult for the players to take to him. They might have forgiven him for his comments in the media – because they were second hand – but when he launched into his rant about them throwing their medals in the bin because they had won them 'by cheating' that finished him in my opinion.

One thing was certain though. His near instant sacking at Leeds worked out far better for Clough than it did for them. And it didn't do me any harm either. I was one of the first to know that Clough was getting the job at Forest before he arrived at the City Ground in January 1975. Edwards phoned me to say that Clough was set to be appointed and that he still wanted me.

This kicked off a strange six months during which I was courted by the most charismatic and brilliant manager of his generation. The way he did it made me feel wanted and determined to play for him months before I ever went to the City Ground to talk terms. First, he sent his scouts up the M1 to watch me play for Donny three times, then he took a look for himself before phoning me to ask if I was interested in playing for Forest. He even joked about blaming me for getting a speeding ticket whilst trying to get to Barnsley in time to watch me!

Playing for Forest wasn't the question. Given a straight choice, I would have gone to a First Division club instead. The real question was 'did I want to play for Brian Clough?' And that was why I went there. Among others who scouted me were Malcolm Allison and Terry Venables of Crystal Palace. Allison was decked out in his famous Fedora hat in the director's box at Darlington when the wooden seat collapsed to the amusement of the fans. Clough knew he had competition and that I would be offered a new deal at Donny. But he told me 'not to sign for anyone else' and found a way to ensure that I didn't miss out money-wise by turning down a new contract.

It was cloak and dagger stuff as Clough sent staff to give me the extra £20! It was literally pushed into my hand in the queue for fish and chips or at The Crown Hotel at Bawtry, near Doncaster. Of course, this wasn't by the book, but it made me feel ten feet tall. The money wasn't as important as the fact that Clough was desperate to sign me.

I met Brian Clough for the first time at a hotel near Nottingham after I'd been to the City Ground to watch Forest with Alan Hill, another Reds' official. We had a very short conversation with Cloughie saying it was nice to see me, but we couldn't be seen in public together as it could be viewed as an illegal approach. On the day that I was due to go to Forest for talks, Donny had lined up meetings with Everton's Billy Bingham, Terry Neill, of Spurs, and Ken Furphy, of Sheffield United, all at Mansfield's Field Mill where Donny reserves were playing. I met Stan Anderson at Belle Vue, Doncaster's ground, and we drove to the chairman's bungalow where he told me not to sign for Forest until I had spoken to all the interested clubs.

We saw Clough at the City Ground. He was there with Forest chairman Brian Appleby, who was dressed in a very smart suit, and Hill. We shook hands and Clough had a contract in his hands and said: 'sign that'.

I said that I wasn't signing anything unless I was in the team on Saturday.

He said 'you're playing'.

"I'll get you promotion," I said.

Then the chairman jumped in: "If you get us promotion, I will buy you a suit."

Forest weren't in the best of shapes. Clough's first few months in charge had been a real struggle as they finished 16th in the Second Division, not far off the drop in a season when Wednesday were relegated. The club had enjoyed some success in the not-too-distant past, winning the FA Cup in 1959 and finishing second in the First Division behind George Best and Manchester United in 1967. But they'd been outside the topflight since 1972, the same season that Clough had steered their bitter rivals Derby to the title. Since then, Derby had won the league again under Clough's successor Dave Mackay and Forest fans were left hoping that the great man could cheer them up.

"Congratulations, young man, you are signing for the champions," he said before money or terms had even been mentioned. I loved his confidence and he loved mine. He told me he was going to turn me into an England player.

"Don't bother, I'll do that myself," I replied.

I was serious about the one condition upon which I signed for him. I wanted to play against Notts County because I wasn't happy to sit on the bench for anyone, not even Brian Clough. The financial part of the deal took about five seconds. He asked me how much I wanted and I said £90 a week, nearly double what

I was offered at Donny. He surprised me by saying he'd pay me £120. Clough smiled and said that he was happy at making this signing and told the chairman he would be also.

That evening Forest were playing at home to Rotherham United in the League Cup and Clough invited me to watch the match. Forest played well and won 5-1 with Martin O'Neill scoring a couple of goals. After the final whistle, Clough told me to follow him into the dressing room to introduce me to my new teammates. We went through the team shaking hands and when he came to O'Neill, he said: "This is the young man who'll be taking your place on Saturday!" I couldn't believe it. Martin never said a word. I thought it was funny, but I wish he hadn't said it. That got me off to a bad start with the lads, including some who had been at the club for a fair time already.

Ironically, I was on the receiving end of the same trick when Gary Mills signed professional terms. The manager introduced Gary to me 'as a player I have signed today who will take your place'. But, unlike Martin, I had my retort.

"He must be a good player," I replied. "Because I know I'm good!"

Clough walked down to the training ground in tracksuit bottoms and a green top, tapping his squash racket at the side of his leg. He looked on from the sidelines, making his points with his voice raised and shouting out instructions to make it clear what he wanted from you. He wanted you to perfect your game and he did genuinely listen to the opinions of the players.

With me, a typical face-to-face chat with Cloughe went something like this: "And what can I do for you today, young man?" He then gave me a chance to say what was on my mind. When I finished, he would say: "Young man, I see your point and you make some good points, but I'm the manager and I make the decisions. Now do what you do best – either score me or create me a goal on Saturday!" He was almost a counsellor in the way he dealt with us. Yes, some players were more fearful of him, but in my view his bark was much worse than his bite. We respected him, so we wanted to do well for him.

Clough laughed with the players on occasions, but was mostly a serious man who kept his distance. That's why many found Clough hard to work out. Former players have often said they didn't know what made the man tick. Well, my opinion is that he kept everything simple. For example, we never practiced dead balls such as free kicks and corners. That was always left to the best players who had the confidence to take them on the pitch.

Clough saw things in players that most missed. I was there when fans had a go at John McGovern, who later became the captain when they won almost all of their trophies. They didn't realise what John gave to the side, but the gaffer did. John did the job he was asked to do. He was very good at making life difficult for the opposition and when he got the ball, he used it quickly and well.

Clough insisted on doing things his way or not at all and had the respect of all the players because he got results. His teams were sometimes criticised for trying to walk the ball into the net, but his ideas made sense. He encouraged us to pass the ball and to look up to find someone in a better position rather than taking a pot shot at goal. He didn't want his full backs lumping the ball into the penalty area just for the sake of it. He had a brilliant player in John Robertson at getting to the byline which makes defending much harder as it turns them around allowing forwards to run onto the ball.

Team talks were about his players, not the opposition. They went something like this: 'Kenny Burns and Larry Lloyd, I pay you to protect the goal - when you get the ball, pass the ball to someone who can play. Peter Withe Tony Woodcock and Gary Birtles, I pay you to score goals, that's your job.' As for Robbo, Martin O'Neill and myself, our job was to run at defenders. He told us they were petrified of us and expected us to chip in with goals ourselves.

Did we see a lot of him at training? No. Did he ever take part in coaching? No. Then on a Saturday we didn't see him in the dressing room until 15 minutes before kick off. Typically he came in swinging his squash racket and sat down next to one of the players to break the ice. Then he quickly give us a few bullet points about what he wanted us to do. No mention of the opposition, he usually sent us out with: "Now go out and show the football world how good you are."

There was never any ranting or raving, but he was very good at picking up on a few points to get more out of us. Clough knew what he wanted from his players and how he could achieve it.

A typical Cloughie pep talk lasted about five minutes whilst some managers spoke for an hour or an hour and a half. Don't get me wrong, there are some players who like to go into things in more detail, but many get bored when given too much information. The boss seemed to know how to approach each individual.

Footballers are no different from any other people - they have their problems whether football-related or in the rest of their life. Being on decent money doesn't alter the need to be listened to – and Clough did that..

Some of the lads commented on how well Clough treated me personally. They thought I was his golden boy as he always praised me to the media. But it was a sign of his man management skills that personal issues didn't affect team selection. He didn't always see eye-to-eye, for example, with Larry Lloyd, one of the players never slow to voice his views. But what he did for Lloydy, discarded by Liverpool then picked up from Coventry for only £50,000, was fantastic. He was almost always in the Forest side which went on to win so many medals.

Cloughie was the same with club staff and even the wives and girlfriends of players who often got bunches of flowers. Whenever he spoke, everyone listened and he got a good response. I can honestly say there was barely a problem with any of the lads when we went away on our many trips. He believed in discipline and we knew how far we could go with him. In some ways being with Clough was similar to being at home with Mum and Dad. The boundaries were set, we were well looked after and knew what was expected of us.

Often after a game on a Saturday and there was no midweek match, he said 'see you on Thursday'. He knew we were match fit and prioritised rest rather than repetitive training routines. We didn't do much physical work on Fridays either, before gathering in the boardroom at lunchtime where the boss hung up the teamsheet. I used to do an impression of him and make him laugh by saying "So who is in the team, young man?"

That's how I describe Brian Clough - the greatest manager I played for. Clough believed in trying to win games rather than not to lose them. He was brilliant at his job and when Clough entered a room everyone stopped and looked. Players and fans feared Clough but respected him for his achievements. Winning two European Cups with a club such as Nottingham Forest speaks for itself. I doubt it will ever be done again.

Almost every other dealing that I had with Clough lived up to the high opinion that I had of him. Cloughie's use of psychology was brilliant, both for our players and referees. He had some top players in the Forest side that I played in and others who were just good. His way was to convince the lads who weren't special that they were better than they actually were. He did this in different ways. One was not to single them out for criticism in the dressing room. If John Robertson and Tony Woodcock were running the show, he was more likely to praise John McGovern and Frank Clark and say that they were holding the team together. The result was that the players became convinced that his judgement of them was right and that we had nothing to fear from the opposition.

Clough's psychology was to convince us that we were better than anyone that we were playing against and therefore our performance was all that mattered. It's surprising how this confidence spreads when a team gets a few positive results. We all know how difficult it is to shake an individual or a team out of a losing rut. Players go onto a pitch worried about the possibility of losing and that affects the way they play. The opposite happens with positive thoughts. Forest players became more and more convinced as their success continued that they were unbeatable – and so it proved for 42 league games, starting in the early months of their First Division title winning season until the following campaign when they were eventually beaten at Liverpool.

Here's a good example of how Clough's psychology helped an individual. John Middleton was an up-and-coming goalkeeper during our promotion season. But he made a few mistakes and there was talk that he wasn't quite ready for the task. We were on the team bus after John had made a mistake in an away game when Clough went up to him and said: "Don't worry about it. You will play for the next eight games!" Imagine how that must have felt and helped a young goalkeeper. Otherwise he would have stepped out at the City Ground the following Saturday thinking one minor slip could cost him his place. Instead, he knew that the manager believed in him enough to guarantee his position.

Yet when he needed to make the change – he did so. After our promotion and a few games in the First Division, the manager recognised that John wasn't the man to help the team win league titles or cups and brought in Peter Shilton. There were three top class goalkeepers in the English game but no way could he get his hands on either, Ray Clemence at Liverpool or Arsenal's Pat Jennings. Shilton, though, was different. He was playing in a struggling Stoke City side that had been relegated from the topflight. Clough faced opposition from Manchester United to sign Shilton and the deal was very nearly done. It is very possible that had that happened United would have been contenders for trophies rather than Forest. There was nothing in Forest's favour other than that Clough offered Shilts more money. The fee of £250,000 was thought by many to be too high for a goalkeeper, let alone his wages, but nobody could argue that he wasn't a bargain.

Clough described Shilton as 'the best goalkeeper in the world' and for most of his time at Forest he played like that. In his first season, he conceded only 18 goals in 37 games as Forest won the title and was voted the Player of the Season by the people who know best – his fellow professionals. The signing of Shilton was a great example of why it was possible for Clough to succeed back then, but it would have been much harder today. The harsh reality in 2021 is that a Peter Shilton would not sign for Nottingham Forest – Clough or no Clough. He would be snapped up by one of the big four because it's impossible for Forest to match their financial resources.

Garry Birtles was a player that Cloughie got far more out of than his ability suggested. When Peter Withe left Forest for Newcastle United, Steve Elliott, who had been banging in the goals in the reserves, was first in line. He didn't score in his first few games, so Clough picked Birtles whom he had signed from Long Eaton United for £2,000. Here was a guy who didn't have real pace or exceptional technique, yet Clough managed to convince him that he was a top, top player.

Birtles has spoken about what it felt like playing under a manager who rated him so highly and not only won medals with Forest but even got three England caps. Yet, as soon as he got his big money move to Manchester United, his bubble burst. He scored his first league goal for United a year after he signed. He was a big fish in a small pond at Forest, pumped up with confidence by his manager and accepted as one of the main lads. At United, it would have been far different. He had to start from scratch and earn respect from his teammates at a superstar club and he couldn't do it. It was no surprise when he returned to Forest and again did well in a team not nearly as good as the one that he'd left.

Clough was very clever when he told us referees had a very difficult job and not to argue with them. He didn't want to risk having the referee against us. He painted a picture that his side played by the rules and a number of officials said they enjoyed doing Forest matches. But, again, he was being clever. He didn't mind Forest players kicking the opposition as long as we picked them up afterwards to make it look like we were the innocent ones.

In one famous interview with John Motson from the BBC, he took *Match of the Day* presenter Jimmy Hill and his colleagues to task for analysing refereeing decisions and highlighting mistakes. It's difficult to prove but I'm sure that referees generally liked Clough and probably fell for the idea that his team were more honest than they were.

The Brian Clough I got to know wasn't the red nosed drinker who made me feel so sad when he led Forest to relegation in his last season. He was smart, sharp and on the ball and I never saw him drunk. Yes, he had a few drinks in our company, particularly when we had something to celebrate, but I never saw him more than merry.

Clough was unpredictable, but not the bully some spoke of, at least not in my presence. Generally, if you were having a difficult time, he'd be your best friend and stick with you. If you needed bringing down a peg or two, it was a different story.

Clough's man management with me was second to none. It showed that he cared about me and my lifestyle, was watching out for me and was prepared to help because ultimately that helped the team. Clough knew that I was quite lonely during my first few months at the City Ground and did his best to keep me on the straight and narrow.

He liked his players to be married because this was a more settled life than chasing women and going to night clubs. I was amazed at how hc always seemed to know what was happening with me when I went home at weekends after Forest matches. He knew where I'd been and who with.

One Monday I thought that I was in big trouble with the manager when I drove into the City Ground for training and he asked for my car keys. Was he looking for evidence of something that I'd done over the weekend? That was on my mind during the training session and walking into his office afterwards to pick up my keys. "There you are," he said, handing me a completely different pair. I couldn't see my car in the car park. "It's over there," said Clough pointing to a new Ford Capri. I couldn't believe it. The manager had been so worried about me clocking up miles on the motorway in my old banger that he bought me a better car. That was amazing.

He was also delighted when he found out I was now dating one girl more often and not being seen out with different ones. He encouraged me to get married to Kim and I did, with Forest captain, John McGovern, as best man. Sad to say, however, that although Cloughie was a huge influence on my life, he couldn't change my nature. I wasn't well suited to married life.

I credit Brian Clough for introducing me to a style of football that changed my life. Only Clough and Bob Paisley at Liverpool had the guts to get the football down and pass it. They were years ahead of their time. Opponents were often beaten before they went on the field. Forest and Liverpool weren't unbeatable but played smarter football.

Clough loved me and treated me very well. When I wanted eight tickets for a Forest match, he gave me them instantly. When others asked, they had to blag a few from their mates. He told me that he knew I was a good player whilst telling others they needed to prove themselves to him. As a young player finding my way at Forest, he showed me unusual kindness to ensure that I felt wanted at the club.

Cloughie taught me how to play football the way I knew it should be played. It took a fair while for it to click at Forest – we only finished 8th in my first season – but he didn't turn to Plan B. His idea was that if Plan A didn't work, try harder until you get it right. His Forest teams all played the same way. His reserve and youth sides knocked the ball along the ground and took the game to the opposition. It meant that young players who came through the ranks like Garry Birtles and Gary Mills fitted into the first team more easily.

He was one of the first managers in English football to realise that you can only get so far by putting the ball into channels and chasing it. He showed us a football in the dressing room and said it was our friend and we should look after it. People didn't always understand him, but in many ways he was years ahead of his time.

People ask whether Cloughie would have made a good England manager and I think he would. He would have given the talented players that we produced in the 1970s and 1980s their chance on the international stage. He would have enjoyed working with the very best and they would have benefitted from his support and trust.

Like Best, Clough had rare charisma and dominated a room – but, unlike Bestie, he never liked small talk or socialising with hangers on. He and I were the perfect fit.

Despite his ordeal at Leeds United and struggling with Brighton before that, the great man was still bursting with confidence. I liked that! The Forest lads respected Clough because he made them into better players and gave them confidence. He never needed to do that with me. I knew from day one that I was as good, if not better, than any opponent that I played against at Forest.

Cloughie even kept Trevor Francis, the first £1m footballer, waiting for his debut, and played him in the third team instead. But he kept his promise to me. I rewarded him by having a very good game against Notts, although somehow we lost the City Ground game 1-0 to a last-minute goal. The Forest team that I joined weren't even champions of Nottingham, but I shared his confidence that they would go on to win trophies.

Everyone knows Cloughie was his own man, but one of the things I liked about him was that he did take on board other opinions. I looked on with interest after I left the City Ground at how John Robertson became one of the best footballers of his generation. Yet he was nearly packed off back to Scotland to sign for Partick Thistle. I had several chats with Clough about both Robbo and Tony Woodcock, who would have gone to Donny had they been able to afford the £20,000 fee. I told the boss to keep both players and that they were very good. History proved me right as they won European Cup medals with Forest and played international football.

Cloughie was again predicting an international career for me – this time publicly – during my second season. In one article he focused on England and Manchester United wingers, Gordon Hill and Steve Coppell, and told the world that I was better! I was full of confidence going into the home game against Burnley and we started like lightning. I got one of the goals as we went 2-0 up in no time. Pre-match, the local press had been speculating about whether we could go one better and score seven after bagging four, five and six against Hereford, Carlisle and Sheffield United in our previous home games. Anything seemed possible.

Then my mate John McGovern played a hospital pass and Paul Fletcher caught me accidentally on the knee. I collapsed in a heap not realising how bad it was. I'd done my cruciate ligaments. Cloughie told the press that evening that 'promotion has just walked out' and that wrecked my career with Forest. I was in hospital for two months and out of the game I loved for four. Even then I probably came back too soon. That was a major, major injury and took the edge off my pace. I often wonder what would have happened had I not suffered that setback.

Clough was joined at Forest by his old sparring partner, Peter Taylor, and I got a good close-up view of one of the most successful and volatile managerial partnerships. When Clough was managing on his own, he wasn't a big smiler. Peter had the ability to make him happier, but they had a lot of arguments. In many ways they were like a husband and wife. They were happier when they were together but couldn't face 24 hours together under the same roof. Taylor made Clough feel more secure. Everyone needs someone who agrees with them on most things and Taylor was that person. Together they knew that they had the potential to win a title at Forest.

Everything was in place for them to go back to Derby, but Clough changed his mind at the last moment. Taylor was disappointed by this because he was a Derby fan and wanted to be there. I wasn't surprised at all that Clough and Taylor ended up falling out spectacularly – in fact, I warned Clough that it would happen!.

The incident which I'm referring to was on our pre-season tour of Germany before the start of the First Division campaign and involved the club's new signing, Kenny Burns. We all knew that Kenny was a bit of a character from his time at Birmingham City. It was also common knowledge that Taylor had done his homework – even following Burns to the greyhound track – to convince Clough that he wasn't that bad. On this occasion Burns had been drinking because he was sitting out the game and was so drunk, he was physically sick. I'd been with Kenny and Taylor blamed me for leading Burns astray. Clough stood up for me by reminding him that I didn't drink. That led to a row between the management team and I quietly told the boss that they would eventually fall out.

Taylor was an insecure man who didn't like to be corrected. There was definitely some jealousy between them. Clough didn't like Taylor getting too much of the credit for their success and the other way around. Taylor had a couple of stabs at managing on his own, at Brighton and Derby, but Clough proved more able to thrive without his right-hand man.

Clough never did take Forest back to the very top after his European Cup winning team broke up, but he built another mostly young side, featuring his son Nigel, Neil Webb, Stuart Pearce and Garry Parker, won a couple more League Cups, finished third in the First Division and reached the FA Cup final against Spurs in 1991. Look where Forest are now – 20 years and counting outside the topflight – to realise just how big an achievement that was.

Clough later took me into his confidence with the story of his final bust up with Taylor. It came after Taylor told Clough that he was retiring after having a heart attack. Without going into the details, Clough helped Taylor out with a couple of personal issues and ensured that everything was in place for him financially to bow out.

Taylor then betrayed Clough's trust by taking the job at Derby. That surprised Clough and made him angry. But worse was to come. Taking John Robertson from Forest to Derby without even talking to Clough was unforgivable in his eyes. Clough felt that he had looked after Robbo at Forest and helped him to become a superstar. In truth, both had helped each other in many ways. But now two people that Clough liked and felt close to had left him without saying a word.

Some people claimed after Taylor's death that they would have made up and Clough said he regretted not doing so. But the truth was that the rift between them was deep and it was very unlikely to happen. We all know how people speak differently after someone has passed away.

I had no contact with Taylor after I left Forest, but Clough was different. As well as chatting personally with me on a number of occasions, he tried three times to lure me back to Forest.

First was when I was at Sheffield Wednesday. I had just ripped Luton Town apart and Jack Charlton was talking about me as a future England player. Clough said that it had been a mistake to sell me, but had let me go because he couldn't let me and Taylor disrupt the team. I said that I wasn't coming back because Wednesday had been promoted and I wanted to help them to get back into the First Division.

Second time was after the tribunal had fixed my transfer to Sheffield United. But this time it was too soon for me to quit Bramall Lane after United chairman Reg Brearley had given me a £50,000 signing on fee – £25,000 in my hand and another £25,000 to be paid when I left the club. He tried again when I finished my loan spell with Everton with a good performance and a 3-1 win over his Forest team. Clough waited for me in the tunnel and once again said that he wanted me back at the City Ground. This time I refused because I knew that Everton were onto something good. Although we were struggling in the bottom half of the First Division when I joined, I knew that the facilities were good and we had some top players. I told Clough that I missed out on trophies when I left Forest and didn't want it to happen again. I also thought that Forest's time had gone and it was unlikely that even Clough could take them back to their former heights.

Clough spoke with me several times on the phone and explained how he fell out with Taylor over transfer issues. He told me Justin Fashanu, Ian Wallace and Peter Ward were all Taylor's signings and that he wasn't happy with any of them. He felt Taylor's standards had dropped and Forest hadn't got good value for money from any of the deals. A bigger club, such as Manchester United or Arsenal, spending £2m or £3m on a few players without getting too much in return might not have been so serious. But at Forest it was a very big setback. This was one of the main reasons that they were unable to sustain their success. Financially, this was always going to be much more difficult for a club of their size.

Clough told me the real story of why he got the police out to evict Justin Fashanu from the training ground. In increasingly politically correct days, Clough took a lot of stick for his handling of Fashanu who had done the very rare thing of coming out as being an openly gay professional footballer. I'll keep what he said to myself, but he was worried about the player's lifestyle and its effect on the club.

Cloughie was as good at managerial mind games as any. I learned a lot from talking with him about his famous and very bitter rivalry with Leeds manager Don Revie. He told me they had a lot of history together as they had been brought up only a few streets apart in Middlesbrough, something most folk don't realise. When I asked why he disliked Revie so much, he explained that when he had been an apprentice manager at Hartlepools he had called on Revie for some advice and was blanked. Like a lot of managers. when he got to the top, Revie looked down on others learning their trade.

Clough never forgot that snub and did everything possible to attack Leeds. The reason was simple – Leeds were a great football team and Clough saw them as rivals. In his TV interviews Clough took every opportunity to spread the idea that Leeds were a dirty side and won matches by cheating. In that well known interview of the two rivals on Yorkshire TV, after Clough had been sacked as manager at Elland Road after only 44 days, he emphasised the differences between them and claimed that he had wanted to win trophies by doing it 'better'. I think the idea that Leeds were much more physical than all their opponents was a clever Clough invention designed to put doubts into people's minds.

Yes, Revie had very strong players not afraid of putting their foot in, but so did other sides. Liverpool built their side on hardmen such as Tommy Smith, Alec Lindsay and Ron Yeats, Chelsea had 'Chopper' Harris and David Webb, and Larry Lloyd and Kenny Burns at Forest were as ruthless as any. Clough did such a good hatchet job on Leeds that some fans still refer to them as 'dirty Leeds' to this day. But he wouldn't have made those comments had they been bottom of the First Division and no threat to his sides.

I was as sad as anyone to see Clough go downhill in that final season which ended with the club being relegated and him looking so ill.

Like George Best, Cloughie conquered so many opponents on the football field, only to be beaten by alcohol. I'm glad that my memories of him were when he was at his brilliant best and I've never forgotten that he showed me the way football should be played.

He singled me out as a young player who he wanted at his football club and we enjoyed a good relationship which not everyone understood. Clough liked me and I liked him. Some may say that was because we were both 'mavericks' although I don't like that term too much. I'd prefer to think that he saw something of himself in me– a talented football man who always did things his own way.

CHAPTER THREE
EVERTON VERSUS SHEFFIELD WEDNESDAY, MAY 14, 1966

BEING voted the Owls' most popular ever player in a Football Focus poll a few years ago was like winning the Ballon D'Or. Hearing my song Singing the Blues over the tannoy at Hillsborough is also very, very special. And I love the banter with fellow Owls fans on social media and, even more, chatting with you in real life.

I think most football fans choose a club and stick with them for life. You can change wives, jobs, where you live, the lot, but not your football team.

My Sheffield Wednesday story began long before I signed for Big Jack and has lasted decades after I left Hillsborough as a player. Being brought up in the Yorkshire village of Kinsley, Barnsley was my nearest professional club and Leeds United the best supported, yet I was always more interested in Wednesday.

The first I remember about the Owls was the match fixing scandal in the early 1960s. A former Mansfield Town player, Jimmy Gauld, was said to have approached Owls player David Layne – the two had played together at Swindon – to fix a match in 1962. Layne then spoke with fellow Owls. Peter Swan and Tony Kay, about throwing a game against Ipswich Town on December 1. He picked this match, it was said, because Ipswich were favourites anyway.

Ipswich won 2-0, Gauld later confessed his sins to a national newspaper in search of more money and the careers of all three Wednesday lads were wrecked. I can well understand Swan's words when he spoke to The Times in 2006. He said: "We lost the game fair and square, but I still don't know what I'd have done if we'd been winning. It would have been easy for me to give away a penalty or even score an own goal. Who knows?"

I came across most things in my career – some of which are in this book, others would get me sued – but was never asked to throw a football match. I wouldn't have done it because it's completely against my nature. Swan did wrong and it cost him the chance to play in one of the biggest games in Wednesday's history, but I get where he was coming from. The only people who can really throw a game are the goalkeepers and the referee.

That's why the match fixing trial, involving Liverpool's Bruce Grobbelaar and Hans Segers, of Wimbledon, at least made sense, even though both were found not guilty by the courts.

If that negative event put Wednesday in my mind, the day I became a supporter was the FA Cup final of 1966. Everton against the Owls was one of the first football matches I watched live on television and was before I started attending games.

The cup final was one of very few football matches broadcast live back then. For a fair while, there was the FA Cup final, European Cup final and England against Scotland – plus England games in World Cup finals. The FA Cup was the most exciting tournament of all. Managers always thought winning the Football League was better, but nothing compared with the magic of the cup.

I supported Wednesday that day as they were the local side – and have never looked back. That was a particularly good Owls line up, one of the best I have seen.

We had a very good goalkeeper. Ron Springett was a Wednesday legend who made more than 300 appearances for the Owls after joining from QPR in 1958. Winning 33 full England caps shows how good he was and he kept goal in the 1962 World Cup finals in Chile. It was only shortly after the FA Cup final that he lost his place in the national team to Gordon Banks, one of the best goalkeepers ever. He was given the number 12 shirt in the squad and watched from the sidelines when Banks and co eventually saw off West Germany 4-2 to win the World Cup at Wembley. Springett served Wednesday well for a decade earning himself a testimonial a year after the FA Cup final

All teams need a rock at centre half and Wednesday's was Peter Eustace, a typical hard, no-nonsense defender, well remembered by many fans. The cup final was in the first of his two spells at Hillsborough and he later became Harold Wilkinson's assistant manager. When Wilkinson jumped ship to go to Leeds, Eustace spent just three months in the top job before being replaced by Ron Atkinson.

My favourite player was in midfield. I always liked Jim McCalliog. He looked after the ball to give himself a bit of space when the game was played at 100 miles per hour. It tells you something about how highly he was rated that, after just a handful of appearances for Chelsea, Wednesday paid the highest transfer fee for a teenager to bring him to Hillsborough - £37,500.

Jim made his mark in his first season for us by scoring in the 2-0 semi final win over his old club at Villa Park and went on to have four years with the Owls before moving onto Wolves. A year after the FA Cup final, Jim scored the winning goal on his debut for Scotland in their famous 3-2 win over England. I played against Jim when he had another successful spell with Lawrie McMenemy's Saints and I was at Forest. He was a Wembley specialist because it was Jim who supplied the killer pass for Bobby Stokes to score the winning goal when Southampton shocked Manchester United in the FA Cup final, a decade after he scored there for us.

Providing fireworks from the right wing was another promising young player in David Ford. The first ever substitute used by Wednesday, he came into his own that season netting 13 goals, including two in the quarter final victory over Blackburn. Putting football into perspective, Ford was involved in a serious car accident in 1967 in which his fiancée lost her life. That was also a major setback in his Wednesday career and he was eventually sold to Newcastle United.

Johnny Fantham was a big goal threat at inside forward and has a place in Wednesday folklore. He netted 166 times for us in a great career, making him our highest post war scorer. Johnny was capable of mixing it with the best, banging in 47 goals in two seasons in the topflight, including one when Wednesday finished second. That goalscoring run earned him a full England cap in 1961. Another player I liked was John Quinn who played in a variety of positions from half back to winger and was an important player for Wednesday after first playing for us in 1959.

It was surprising that Wednesday only finished 17th in the First Division that season, six places behind mid-table Everton as manager Harry Catterick slowly built a side who eventually became title winners. The game itself was fantastic, one of the best cup finals I remember, but summed up my life-long experience of being an Owls fan. It was a case of so near, yet so far and that's been so for most of the last 55 years.

Wednesday got themselves into a great position with Jim McCalliog netting after four minutes and David Ford putting us into a 2-0 lead in the second half after Gordon West half saved a shot by Fantham. West was a Yorkshireman I never met, but I was a friend of his brother.

As an 11-year-old I didn't know as much about football as I do now, but everyone will tell you about being 2-0 up and how a game can turn when the opposition get a goal back. I go mad when teams sit back and try to manage a game, giving the ball to the opposition. I want to see my team continue doing what got us into such a good position. It's harder for teams to come back if they are spending time defending their own goal.

The Toffees got themselves back into the cup final within two minutes with a well-taken goal by a young lad called Mike Trebilcock. That changed the flow of the game and soon afterwards Trebilcock got himself a second before a slip by Wednesday allowed Derek Temple to run clear and place his shot past Springett. There was time for a pitch invader and a late wasted Wednesday chance, but when the final whistle went I was heartbroken.

There were 100,000 in the crowd that day, including John Lennon and Paul McCartney of The Beatles, and a few tears shed back in Kinsley. I cheered myself up by taking a football to the local field with my brother Dave. I was Jim McCalliog and he was Peter Osgood, his favourite player, and we both banged in a few goals.

I scored goals for Kinsley Boys as I dreamt of being a professional footballer and washed cars and cleaned windows to get enough money to go with my mates, Mickey Appleton and Stephen Jones, to watch my Wednesday heroes at Hillsborough. We loved being on the packed kop. Adults allowed us down at the front to get a better view. I went about a dozen times a season and remember seeing Manchester United, Manchester City, Arsenal, Wolves and other big clubs. I was thinking 'this is going to be me one day' as Sheffield Wednesday got into my blood.

I was disappointed when Owls were relegated from the First Division in 1969/70 and were beginning to struggle in the Second Division as I was taking my first steps as a professional footballer with Doncaster Rovers.

My relationship with Wednesday then changed as I concentrated on my own career. But theirs was the first result I looked out for on the videoprinter on the TV or on the radio in the players' lounge. Sometimes I waited for the Green Un newspaper, but Saturday wasn't over until I knew how Owls had got on. My interest in Wednesday was well known at Donny.

It was strange that I never ever played against Sheffield Wednesday. Mostly my clubs were never in the same division. Probably the closest I came was when I signed for Second Division Forest the summer after Owls had been relegated to the Third.

I felt the pain like all Wednesday fans. We are a big, big club - three-times winners of the FA Cup, have mostly been in the First Division and play at a great ground. Yet in 1975 we reached the lowest point in our proud history.

It almost got worse. Len Ashurst's team avoided going down to Division Four on the last day of the 1975-76 season with a 2-1 win over Southend United who were relegated instead. Owls were second bottom and three points adrift of safety with three games left before scraping two wins and a draw.

The first hint of light came when Ashurst was replaced by Big Jack in October 1977 around the time I was going to Derby County. I knew he could help us. Big Jack had started well as a manager getting Middlesbrough promoted as Division Two champions, then settling them into life in Division One. He had even applied for the England job after Revie jumped ship. It was a coup for Wednesday to get him to manage in Division Three.

For highlights of my three years at Owls with Big Jack, see Part Two. I only wish that he had taken my word and improved our Second Division team whilst I was there. After I left, he signed a quality defender in Mike Lyons, from Everton, and took Owls to the top of the league before they faded to finish sixth. In my opinion, Howard Wilkinson got us promoted on the back of Big Jack's hard work.

CHAPTER FOUR
GOLDEN YEARS TO ROCK BOTTOM

MY best years as a Wednesday fan were when Ron Atkinson and Trevor Francis were in charge. I always rated Big Ron for turning West Brom into one of the most entertaining and successful teams in the land and from his time at Manchester United. I wish that he had stayed longer at Hillsborough both times when he got the job.

Big Ron's first task was to get Wednesday out of a relegation battle after Howard Wilkinson left and Peter Eustace's difficult time in the job. The way that the 1989/90 season ended with a 3-0 defeat at Hillsborough against Forest taking us back down into the bottom three was one of my most gutting times as a 'Wednesdayite'. Ron had got the side playing well again and with a few games to go we looked in little danger.

One of the turning points was a late defeat by Tottenham Hotspur. We were leading 2-1 and heading towards a spot in the top half of the table. Yet we went on to lose 3-2. There was nothing we could do about Luton Town's good run but Big Ron would have told the lads to ignore what was happening elsewhere and to concentrate on getting the job done against Forest.

We only needed a draw to make totally sure of staying up but anything can happen if you are still in danger on the last day. Playing against a mid-table side was in our favour but not Forest. Brian Clough never allowed his teams to think like that. Stuart Pearce got a couple of goals and Nigel Jemson, who later enjoyed some success at Wednesday, bagged the other.

The way Wednesday bounced back the following season when we got promoted and won the League Cup against Manchester United at Wembley was outstanding. Again, inspired by Big Ron, we played very good, attacking football and it was one of the proudest days of my life as an Owls fan when we landed a trophy.

Winning the League Cup was a far bigger deal in those days and Wednesday's triumph was far from a fluke. We matched Fergie's side on the day and John Sheridan's brilliant goal sent us all into dreamland.

Exactly what we would have done in the topflight under Big Ron we will never know, but I understand why he left for Aston Villa. As a player who left Southampton to go to Wednesday because they were my club, I can't blame Big Ron when he got the chance to manage a club that he thought a lot of. He left us, though, in very good hands under Trevor Francis before we became our own worst enemy when Dave Richards harshly sacked him.

The Francis years in charge at Hillsborough saw good coaching and he was backed to bring in very good players. Perhaps it was the one who got away that stood between us moving to the next level and becoming a trophy-winning team.

I liked what I saw of Owls during that time under Francis, although some of the feedback that I got was that the manager was quite aloof from the players. I get the impression that some of the lads liked him and others didn't. The Trevor Francis that you saw on TV looked relaxed and comfortable, but he wasn't the kind of man who liked talking to the press. They can make life awkward at times and will get managers sacked. It's always a plus for the manager to try to get the media on his side, rather than against him.

There were some notable near misses during Trevor's time, including finishing third in the First Division in his first season and getting to the final of both the FA Cup and League Cup the following year. Looking back on it, finishing third was probably his best achievement but the cup runs were more exciting. Wednesday played some very good football and had a world class player in Chris Waddle.

I rated both Waddle and John Barnes as world class at that time. They would have been rated even more highly had they played with teammates of the same ability. Had they been French or Spanish, they might have been looked on as superstars.

As it turned out, Waddle's international career was already over, but the form that he showed with Owls should have made him an England regular. One of my favourite Waddle memories is of him showing Ryan Giggs a trick or two near the touchline in a match against United. To be honest, I don't remember him having a bad game when I saw him for Wednesday.

There were very good players in that Wednesday side, including a couple of my former Forest teammates. Viv Anderson was an outstanding full back with the ability both to defend and get forward and goalkeeper Chris Woods also followed in Peter Shilton's footsteps with England.

We had a very good balance in midfield. I always thought that Carlton Palmer was a better footballer than many gave him credit for. He took a lot of stick when Graham Taylor put him in the England side, but for Wednesday he was an asset. He was strong and tough, with an engine to get up and down the pitch. For me, he was the ideal holding midfield player to give the ball to Shez who had the skills to unlock defences. We also had Graham Hyde, who had come through the ranks, in that area of the pitch.

Waddle, of course, was outstanding in the cup finals in 1993 against Arsenal, which we could easily have won, and also in the FA Cup semi final against The Blades. That in some ways was a cup final because it was not only a clash of two bitter rivals, but was also at Wembley in the early days when the semi finals were played there.

Waddle got us off to a great start by netting a brilliant free kick and we managed to edge the tie 2-1, thanks to Mark Bright's second half winner. I did expect us to beat United as we were the better side, but credit to them that they played quite well at Wembley and gave us a hard tie.

Arsenal were always going to be tough and to get them in both finals was even tougher. I think anyone who watched the three games, including the FA Cup replay, would agree that there was nothing really between the two sides. Yet it was Arsenal who got their hands on both sets of silverware.

The player who got away was Eric Cantona. Perhaps this was one step too far for Francis. Nobody doubted the Frenchman's ability. But could the manager have handled him? We will never know. The facts of the matter are that we had him on trial at Hillsborough and didn't snap him up. Instead, he went to Leeds United where he starred in Howard Wilkinson's title-winning side before his incredible time at Manchester United. Had Cantona gone to Wednesday, we could have been a Leeds or a United.

The best managers, such as Cloughie and Sir Alex, were always up for the challenge of handling a top player. I never met him, but I saw enough of Cantona on and off the field to know that he was a character. Most players keep quiet whether they agree with a manager or not, Cantona would say his piece. That requires confidence and man management to handle. A Cantona has got to know that the manager is in charge. Sir Alex had that ability and got the best out of him even after his kung fu kick at Crystal Palace. Can you imagine a Wednesday forward line of Eric Cantona, Chris Waddle and Paolo Di Canio, with Benito Carbone in the wings?

Finishing seventh and 13th in the First Division in the next two seasons wasn't great after Francis' early success, but I still think Wednesday made the wrong decision to sack him.

I was quite encouraged by the appointment of David Pleat, who was known for playing good football and brought in brilliant Italian duo, Paolo Di Canio and Benito Carbone. He briefly took us to the top of the league in 1996 before we finished a respectable seventh. But he was sacked after a terrible start to the following season when we won only one of our first 17 games.

Again, we had a chance to sort things out when Big Ron returned to steady the ship. They always say 'never go back' but Ron Atkinson was good enough and confident enough to be an exception to that rule. He more than did his job by keeping us up that season.

But what happened next was another example of mismanagement at Hillsborough. I have asked myself the question many times over: did Richards bring back Ron Atkinson in order to sack him; in other words, to get revenge for when Big Ron gave his word that he was staying at Wednesday then moved to Villa? I can't think of any other reason why he didn't keep Big Ron after he had saved us. That played a big part in Wednesday slipping out of the big time, never so far to return.

I knew Danny Wilson from his early playing days at Bury. He is a very nice bloke who had a good playing career and went on to do reasonably well in management but not strong enough to do the job that we needed.

It wasn't Danny's fault that Di Canio pushed referee Paul Alcock after being sent off against Arsenal in September 1998, or that the Italian was suspended for 11 matches. But I contrast the way that Danny dealt with the issue with how Sir Alex handled Eric Cantona's long suspension.

Fergie would never allow that serious incident to weaken his team and got Cantona back into the fold. Danny got rid of Di Canio and that led to relegation. I know how things work in football and Di Canio's departure would have had a big effect on Carbone who wasn't the same force in our relegation season. Just look at what Di Canio did for West Ham. He was brilliant. Wednesday went down by five points. Had he stayed, I'd have backed him to get us another ten.

There was talk of splits in the Wednesday dressing room between the British and the foreign players – again I can't prove it. But Richards and co. should have done more to help. Peter Shreeves did a reasonable job as caretaker manager to keep us in with an outside chance of staying up until the last but one match, but we should have hired someone permanently.

The result was that we went down when we were getting ourselves into mounting debt. You can deal with that in the Premier League, but it becomes more difficult when you go down into the Championship as many big clubs have found to their cost.

I only wish that I could write something to cheer up fellow Owls fans about what has happened since and what is still happening now – but I can't.

The last 20 years have been a disaster for the football club that I love and after the 2020/21 season we are back to rock bottom. A season with no fans allowed to watch was difficult and horrible for many reasons, but we made it even worse by appointing Tony Pullis.

Nothing against the man personally – he might be the nicest guy in the world – but, for me, Pullis highlights much that is wrong about English football. We have managers and coaches at club and international level who don't take us forward. They play safety-first defensive football – aiming not to lose – and end up winning nowt!

Pullis was just one of a long list of managers given the task of taking us back to the top league – and failing. They have all, except Carlos Carvalhal, been quite similar. In my opinion, all we did was bring in a long ball manager and waste even more time. Look where we are now!

For the first time in 50 odd years, I wasn't bothered about watching my club play football. Now we are back in League One, a million miles away from the Premier League. When I joined Owls as a player, I thought that we were getting ourselves out of Third Division football for good. I would never have believed that in the first few years of the 21st century we'd go back down there, not once, but three times.

The real problem at Hillsborough runs deeper than any manager. It lies with the owners and the way that our great club is run. You can say the same about any club that is failing. The buck really stops with the people who appoint managers and make the other key decisions.

Pullis was our 15th full time manager since 2000. So it can't be all their fault. I look at the full list of managers that Wednesday have appointed in the last 20 years and they don't excite me. None were good enough to get us back into the Premier League and for us to stay there. Time and time again we have gone for safe options and gone round in the same circles. That was never going to end with Pullis. We deserve better than appointing managers who concentrate on getting the team organised, work on defensive drills and play boring long ball football.

We have only really challenged at the top end of the Championship under Carvalhal. That was the last time I was impressed with what I saw at Wednesday. We played some attractive football, reaching the play offs in successive seasons and had Carlos been a little more adventurous against Huddersfield we may well have got ourselves promoted.

Perhaps Carlos had run out of gas after three years at Hillsborough? That's possible, but what has happened since doesn't make for good reading.

Steve Bruce did quite well during his few months in charge, although I can't say that I'm a fan of his football either. Watching two of my old clubs when Wednesday beat Forest 3-0 at Hillsborough, I kept asking myself how Bruce, who was schooled by Sir Alex at United, and Martin O'Neill, who played for so long under Cloughie, could produce such poor football?

Jos Lukahay simply wasn't good enough for the job, then Garry Monk was found out. When I look back on the managers who have come and gone, there's one inevitable question: should the managers have been given more time?

It's always a hard one when things aren't going well. Looking back into my playing career, Cloughie took a while to turn things around at Forest and Howard Kendall was on the verge of being sacked at Everton before things changed completely. I think managers can be sacked too quickly in modern day football but, Carvalhal aside, I can't make a case for recent Owls bosses.

Instead of going for average British managers, we should be getting the advice of the best in the business, such as Pep Guardiola and Jurgen Klopp, to recommend a coach who plays the right way and has something about them. Then we could start to build something, rather than chopping and changing so that managers can make excuses, such as the players aren't fit or good enough and it's not his team. I want to see someone with vision and coaching ability, someone with the skill and clout to bring in better players and improve the existing ones.

With one or two exceptions, such as Steven Gerrard and Frank Lampard, English managers usually aren't the answer. Ok, Owls have had mixed success with foreign bosses so far, but we are still more likely to get success with someone who hasn't been on an FA coaching course.

I want to be wrong, but the club I love is in a mess. We no longer own the ground; we go from manager to manager and we're playing in a division that we shouldn't be in.

In my view it was harsh that the team and the fans suffered from the alleged financial wrongs over the ground. I think that, as with other clubs, including Wigan, in the previous season, the people responsible should be penalised rather than having a points deduction. Luckily the 12 points were reduced to six but that put us on the back foot even before the kick off 2020/21 season.

Instead of trying to somehow get out of a hole, we need to build for the future and play football suited to the Premier League when we ever get there. Playing that way will attract better players. Bielsa has done it with Leeds United, Wednesday have equally as much potential in my opinion. As Big Ron says, Wednesday fans are fantastic and there are 30,000 plus out there, just longing to get behind a team that they can be proud of.

If my time in football has taught me anything it is that I should be surprised at nothing. I hope my Wednesday love affair has a happy ending, not only for my sake but for all long-suffering Owls.

Sheffield Wednesday are one of the biggest and best clubs in the country. Always have been, still are. They should be in the Premier League at the very least and potentially challenging, if not for the title itself, at least a European place.

Why it's not happened for us since I fell in love with them back in 1966, I can't honestly tell you. I haven't been in the boardroom when key decisions have been made – such as the decisions to stick with a manager or sack him, to give him the money to make big signings or to withhold it because they never really trusted him.

So instead, here's my best ever Wednesday team from my lifetime of supporting them. This lot would put a smile on our faces.

It won't surprise you that there's no place for anyone over the last 20 years. The most recent who gets into my team is big David Hirst. I hope that you enjoy this Wednesday team. We all have our opinions and you may disagree but here goes . . .

Goalkeeper Ron Springett

Ron was my first ever Owls goalkeeper – and the best. He wasn't the biggest goalie in the world at 5'9" but he was agile and very brave. Ron was in goal when Owls finished second to that great Spurs side in 1961 and stayed with us until 1967 when he was replaced by his younger brother, Peter, who was also a very good goalkeeper. One thing that I learnt from Brian Clough that has stayed with me all my life - you don't win anything in football without a quality keeper. RIP Ron.

Right back: Ronald Nilsson

I'm a big fan of foreign players and what they have brought to English football. We've had our fair share at Hillsborough and not all have been good for the team, either on and or off the field. This lad, however, was class. We were struggling near the bottom of the First Division and struggling for a reliable full back when Big Ron brought Nilsson in from Sweden.

He was a fantastic player in my opinion. I like to see a full back good on the ball and willing to get forward on the overlap to cause the opposition problems. But you must be good defensively too. Nilsson was that. He knew when to attack and when to stay back because he read the game very well. Nilsson was a key part of Ron's side that won promotion back to the First Division and landed the League Cup. And he was still with us when Trevor Francis led us to both cup finals. When Vital Football asked Wednesday fans who the best right back in Wednesday's history was, they chose Nilsson – you got it spot on! Probably the best foreign player in our history – so far!

Centre back – Peter Swan

Was a great player for Wednesday and could have been even greater but for the betting scandal. He was the centre half in the Alan Hanson, Mark Lawrenson and Phil Thompson mould. Technically brilliant, he could bring the ball out from the back when others lump and hump it. He had made 19 successive appearances for England before he was ill and missed the 1962 World Cup finals in Chile. I think he could have made the ideal partner for Bobby Moore in 1966. Sorry Big Jack! Did come back and play a few games for Owls after his lengthy ban, but by then his career was all but over. More than happy to have him in my side though.

Centre back – Mark Smith

A local boy come good, Mark was in the same team as me at Wednesday, so I know what a player he was. He was my kind of defender – got stuck in without selling himself in the tackle, didn't panic on the ball and good enough to get the team moving forward. He was at Hillsborough for ten years and part of two promotion sides. Was also a better penalty taker than most forwards. Always happy to take responsibility, a player you'd want in your team rather than the opposition, that's for sure.

Full back – Peter Rodrigues

Technically gifted, Rodrigues had the fitness to keep going up and down the flank and the ability to find an end product. He wasn't a full back who put the ball 'into an area' for the opposition to head it out, he crossed a good ball for a striker to get on the end of. Had already played in the First Division for Leicester City and become a regular in the Welsh national team before he joined us and had four out of five good seasons at Hillsborough. Was a loss to us when the team was struggling and he was snapped up on a free transfer by Southampton Then towards the end of his career he was good enough to play in their famous FA Cup final win over Manchester United in 1976.

Holding midfield – John Sheridan

Cloughie's loss was our gain! After being very popular with Leeds United fans, Clough snapped him up, then moved him on without even playing a league game. No idea why that happened but he was a fantastic player for Wednesday. Shez was a ball player. Always had that bit of time to get the ball under control and the composure not to rush but play it forward at the right moment. He was a quality player because he understood the game and took part in some memorable games for us. It was his rocket shot that won the League Cup against Manchester United and he was in the side that so nearly brought home both cups a couple of years later. Never asked Cloughie why he didn't fancy Shez – but glad he didn't!

Right midfield – Jimmy McCalliog (captain)

My favourite ever Wednesday player and I've seen a few great ones over the years. Should have had more than five full caps for Scotland. I never really got the chance to tell Jimmy how highly I rated him, so I'm doing it here. No need to say any more here than that he was a top, top player.

Left midfield – Ante Mirocevic

If ever a player summed up the frustrating side of Big Jack, it was Mirocevic. Some say we never saw the best of him at Hillsborough and it's easy to know why. He was a ball player, a lad with skill who could supply the forwards, but Big Jack's methods never suited him. Didn't speak much English when he joined us, but I invited him to my house – like I did most Wednesday signings – and got on with him. Like Shez, he understood football and that was more important than the language. Could find a bit of space and then provide a quality pass. A Yugoslavia international, Ante would have benefitted from playing for Wednesday when we were in the First Division and had better players. His goal against Brighton in our losing FA Cup semi final of 1983 was a reminder of what might have been.

Right attack – Paolo Di Canio

The Italian has a lot of the qualities I want from an attacking player. Yes, he was temperamental but I'm judging his ability. He created and scored goals, won space by pulling people out of the position and scared opposition managers. Interchanging flanks with Waddle in this team, he would cause havoc. If only he had stayed at Hillsborough longer than he did. . .

Centre forward – David Hirst

Must be a great player to keep Johnny Fantham out of my team and Hirstie was. Legend with Owls fans over 11 seasons despite Alex Ferguson trying again and again to take him to Manchester United, Hirstie had a bit of everything as a striker. Brave as an ox, his willingness to put his head and leg in to try to nick a goal probably contributed to his list of injuries. Like Andy Gray at Everton in that way. But he also had a lot of skill and a ferocious shot. Couldn't have done too much more for Wednesday – even played in goal once. But how many goals would he have scored had he got the creative abilities of Di Canio and Waddle alongside him?

Left attack – Chris Waddle

Cloughie once said of Trevor Brooking 'he floats like a butterfly and stings like one'. Waddle could never be accused of that. He had brilliant skills and flair, but he would also put tackles in and make a big effort for the team. In my view Chris Waddle was a brilliant footballer – would walk into the England team today. At times at Hillsborough he was completely unplayable. He wasn't just man of the match in the FA Cup and League Cups finals against Arsenal, he was the best player on that pitch by a mile. I'd have loved to have played in the same team as him.

Player Manager – Terry Curran

Even though I liked Big Ron as a manager and the way his teams played, I'd have loved to have managed this team with my philosophy. We'd have played with a tempo, movement to create space for each other and take on defenders. This would get fans off their seats. Hillsborough would be rocking with the likes of Di Canio, Waddle and Hirst running riot and the swagger and arrogance of Shez, the master, pulling the strings and seeing the decisive pass. This team would pass and look after the ball and entertain our great supporters playing 4-3-3. I'm also the super sub in my dream team, ready to come on and give the Hillsborough fans an extra thrill if that is possible.

PART TWO
MY FOOTBALL CAREER

CHAPTER ONE
GOING INTO AND OUT OF
THE FOREST

By Alan Hill, former assistant manager of Nottingham Forest

TERRY CURRAN signing for Forest was an interesting story. This is how I remember it. We had been tipped off about Terry at Doncaster Rovers and he played well when I went with scout Maurice Edwards to watch him. So Brian Clough watched him and told Terry not to sign a new contract because he wanted to sign him at the end of the season.

We found out that Terry was offered another £20 a week to stay at Donny, so sent Maurice Edwards to meet him at The Crown Hotel at Bawtry and pay him the extra £20. Imagine how that would look in today's game!

He stayed with us at the Forest Hills Hotel for a while after he signed and he was playing really well. Terry was a likeable lad and got on very well with the boss. He always had an argument with the boss and Cloughie liked that.

His knee injury was very unfortunate. If that hadn't have happened, he would probably have stayed with Forest longer. I lost contact with him after he went but he had a very good career with Sheffield Wednesday and Everton.

*****

By Steve Kindon, former Burnley and Wolves striker

NOTTINGHAM FOREST became a great team winning the First Division title, then the European Cup the next two years. The best player in that team was their left winger John Robertson.

But when Wolves came to the City Ground in August 1976 there was one Forest player on the mind of our manager Bill McGarry – and it wasn't Robertson.

Terry Curran was part of Bill's Fab Four. There were only three other opposition players who he picked out for special attention whilst I played under him in both the First and Second Division and Terry was in good company. They were Kevin Keegan at Liverpool, Trevor Francis when he was at Birmingham and Leeds United's Tony Currie.

With all of them, the boss told us that each time we lost the ball we needed to get a player close to their main threat. That way we would stop them getting the ball to someone who could do us damage.

Terry was playing on the right wing that afternoon at the City Ground but was almost totally two footed. We knew he could cut inside on his left foot as well as going down the line. Things went well for us as we won 3-1 on the way to both sides getting promotion back to the topflight.

But Terry Curran was a super player. There weren't that many players exciting enough to get fans off their feet, but he was one of them, along with the others McGarry told us of and, to a lesser extent perhaps, Steve Kindon.

Like Terry, I'd push the ball yards beyond the full back and race onto it. There'd be 'oohs' from the crowd. They enjoyed watching what was always a good dual between players like Terry Curran and the full back.

A few years later I was commercial manager at Huddersfield Town when Terry came to play for The Terriers. He wasn't always at his best, ast he was towards the end of his career and struggling with injuries.

I watch football now and the players are bigger and more skilful. But the end product isn't necessarily better. The best teams like Manchester City, Liverpool and Barcelona, for several years, pass, pass, pass and the crowd applaud when they pass it into the *net. Teams hunt more in packs and it has become more a game of mobile chess with the result being easy to predict in about 70 per cent of cases.*

There isn't so much room for characters – and the game is poorer for it. Terry Curran was one of those characters, no doubt about it.

*****

I HAD a terrific career as a footballer from 1973 to 1988 and loved almost every minute of it. I won a First Division title winning medal, played at Wembley, became an idol at the club I have supported all of my life and left a lot of happy memories. Even now at 66 years old, there's no shortage of people either in real life or social media to remind me of my career.

Managers such as Brian Clough, Lawrie McMenemy and Jack Charlton described me as an England player. Why that never happened was partly down to me and partly things outside of my control. But none of it was due to a lack of talent or self-confidence.

The cruciate ligament injury that I suffered at Nottingham Forest when I was beginning to tear defences apart was a huge factor. That injury has ended careers and it limited mine far more than I realised at the time. Wednesday fans remember me for being quick, but I was like lightning when I played for Brian Clough.

A mystery injury at Everton then severely limited my appearances for Howard Kendall's great team. I was out of the side for months and some even thought I was winging it – which was never me – until it was finally diagnosed as a thigh problem. I would have given anything to have been fit enough to play a bigger part in one of the best sides that Britain has produced.

The rest was down to me. I never stayed anywhere for more than three years because I disagreed with how some managers played the game. I knew what I wanted and how the game should be played and refused to accept anything less.

But the list of 15 clubs that you see beside my name on Wikipedia is misleading for half were always meant to be short term. I had a couple of spells abroad, including when I was still on Wednesday's books and I finished my career by doing a series of favours for managers I knew when my legs were all but knackered.

Twice I dropped down to the Third Division. I'll never regret playing for the Owls, but I should have listened to my mate Alan Ball who gave me a very good tip at Southampton. He said that I had the pace, aggression and skill to have a long career in the topflight and could play for England but needed to tone down the way that I spoke with managers.

I never accepted being dropped which resulted in me leaving the best two managers that I played for – Cloughie and Howard Kendall. The way I looked at it – if I wasn't in the team on the Saturday, I wanted away. Bally and Cloughie both told me to have more patience and that I would always get back into the first team. I wish now that I had taken more notice.

But I can honestly tell you this – I never gave less than 100 per cent for anyone when I crossed that white line. BBC commentator Barry Davies said I 'could play when I want to' after I scored one of the goals of my life for Wednesday against Sheffield United at Bramall Lane. He was wrong! I always wanted to play, but sometimes I wasn't allowed to. The opposition doubled up on me, cut the supply line and kicked me out of games. Also my teams, including Wednesday, lumped it long for me to chase rather than give me service.

I'm not proud that I left Wednesday to go to Sheffield United and that guaranteed me plenty of stick from their supporters when they weren't winning. Even at Bramall Lane, when I was desperate to go back to Everton, I tried my heart out. That's me. I know no other way.

I was brought up the hard way and wanted to win. I laugh when people talk about 'white privileges'. I had none and had to work for everything that came to me. I was brought up as one of seven brothers – John, Peter, Terrence (the real Terry!), Alan, Bernard, Dave and myself – in a two up two down house in Kinsley. Melvyn, the youngest, followed later.

Most of the boys slept in the same bed, in a house with no central heating and a coal fire with a two-ring oven for cooking and heating up the water for the tin bath. In winter it was absolutely freezing with six-inch icicles on the window. Could have been worse. At least my parents owned the house and Dad had a car.

Mum and Dad gave us all that they could in times when everyone had to work hard for anything they got. It was difficult, but the sort of upbringing that toughened me up for the world of football where young lads sink or swim.

My father was the most important and best person in my whole life. He worked all his life down the pit until his hand became paralysed and he got what I call a 'button job' at the mine. Dad passed his shoes down to me. After two or three weeks of wear, they had holes in them which Dad stuffed with cardboard. My socks were wet through when I got to school.

David and I were very competitive. We always had a ball and tried to beat each other. Summer holidays were our best times. We played outside all day from 7am to 10pm, only coming home for lunch and tea. There weren't any worries as people in the village looked after each other.

The way David and I ran against each other set the pattern for what happened when I was training with professional footballers. I wasn't a bad long distance runner – but David was better over a shorter distance; but he couldn't live with me, any more than the pros could. I was always very quick.

Things got a little more comfortable when we sold the house and moved to a four-bedroom council house in Tonbridge Crescent. I slept in my own camp bed and life was better for us.

David and I practised our football skills in the ginnels. Ask anyone who knew us back then and they'll tell you that I wasn't the best footballer in the family. David was the most talented – a striker who knew where the back of the net was. In one season alone, playing on a Saturday and a Sunday, he scored an amazing 208 goals He had a chance to play for Forest and Sheffield Wednesday but, after a few days at Doncaster Rovers, decided that professional football wasn't for him.

Peter was also a good centre forward but even better as a goalkeeper. I loved watching him keep goal for Kinsley Boys. He was known as 'the cat' and could have signed for Barnsley.

The West Yorkshire villages of Kinsley, where I was born, and Fitzwilliam and the town of Hemsworth, where I live now, are so close to one another that they're almost a three-in-one. It amazes me how many footballers and sportsmen in general have come from this very small area over the years. But, more than that, there have been endless lads who could have made it in professional football.

The first club that I played for was Kinsley Boys and I started banging in goals for the Bantams from an early age. I was good enough to play against lads a little bit older and enjoyed being a striker who thought mostly about how many goals that I could score.

Just before I arrived on the professional scene, there were 'locals' such as brothers, Cyril and Peter Knowles, who played for Spurs, John Radford, a striker in Arsenal's double winning side in 1971 and defender Jeff Clarke, of Newcastle United and Sunderland.

I have never had the chance to meet John or Jeff, but I knew a little more about the Knowles' brothers. Peter was a fantastic footballer who could have been a national and international superstar. He was a very successful forward with Wolves and even bigger things were being predicted about him when he quit football at the age of 24 or 25 to become a Jehovah's Witness.

I saw Cyril play when some of my mates picked me up from Doncaster to watch a match at Anfield between Liverpool and Spurs. It was there that I got Cyril's autograph along with those of Mike England and Martin Chivers.

Others locals who played professionally included Dean Barrick, of Wednesday, Rotherham and Donny, Sam Collins, of Huddersfield, Hull and Hartlepool, and Andy Holdsworth, best remembered at Huddersfield.

This area is also home to one of the most famous cricketers of all time in Sir Geoffrey Boycott, who was brought up in Fitzwilliam. I often went past his family home, but never met him. I've got a feeling that he knew all about me.

Boycott was a big friend of Cloughie's and I think it was either him or one of his mates who kept a look out for me for the boss when I was at Forest. Clough seemed to know more about what I'd been up to at the weekend than I did and said I drove more miles than James Hunt!

There was also rugby league in my family background as Mum's cousin, Billy Batten, was a legend. He was a great player for Great Britain, England, Hunslett and Hull during the early 20th century and so popular among Hull fans that they printed 'Battern certain to play' over posters promoting home matches at The Boulevard. Billy headed a family of top players in what is very much a rugby league area. His sons Eric, Rob and Billy Junior were all professionals along with Billy Junior's son Ray, who played for Leeds, England and Great Britain.

But the real reason that I'm writing this is to tell you about some names that you aren't familiar with – lads of real footballing talent who didn't go on to play professionally. In my time alone there were plenty. I know I was good, but some others were even better. The difference between a young lad, who makes it into the professional game and one who doesn't, is more to do with discipline and attitude than talent.

When I was 17 or 18 I missed out on Friday and Saturdays nights out with the lads. Most teenagers like to go out drinking, but I never went down that road. Alcohol was never a big thing in our family although Dad enjoyed his Stout. Even now, most of us aren't that bothered about it.

It's possible to let your hair down and have some social life once you're established as a footballer – but, today, they are likely to find their every move is being tracked. Thank God there were no mobile phones in my day!

You must put football first if you want to go further. I think that was why lads such as Graham, Peter and Mel Norbury, Barry Smith, Eddie and Paddy Connelly, Tony Wilson, Paul Hornsby, Chalkie White, Oliver Lewins and Lenny Barrack never followed me into the professional game. Good luck to them – everyone makes their own decisions.

Signing professional forms with Doncaster Rovers at the age of 18 was big for me. The day I 'made it'. I scored bags of goals in village football, played a few trial games and then it happened. Donny's manager, Maurice Setters, gave me my first big chance with a team struggling near the bottom of the Fourth Division.

I owe Doncaster Rovers a lot. After my playing days were over, it was great to go back and do some coaching with their academy sides. There I helped my son, Jock, to take his first steps towards what I hope will be an equally enjoyable career in professional football.

Nothing that happened afterwards could have taken place without Setters and his team having faith in me. There are many young lads left on the scrap heap for all sorts of reasons. I was one of the lucky ones.

I was going into a glamorous and exciting world, but Belle Vue was perfect to keep my feet on the ground. The place was almost falling apart and the dressing room full of battle-hardened pros doing their best to ensure that the team didn't crack with it. Everyone dreaded being demoted out of the Football League and for Donny it was becoming an annual battle.

Defender John Haselden taught me one of my first lessons. I was sorry to hear early in 2020 that John had passed away after suffering from Alzheimer's for the last few years of his life. But back then, the very sight of him made me laugh. Watching the rugged defender hobble out of the bath, I couldn't stop myself from making some smart comments. He was about 30 but looked 65. "Wait until you're 30," he said. "You won't be laughing then."

Too right, mate. My body was knackered from taking the same kind of physical knocks as John. We played at different ends of the pitch, but I was a brave footballer who never shirked a challenge. Now I walk with a limp, my ankle has been pinned and my knees are a wreck.

My Football League debut was an early reality check. I was excited about getting the nod to start at Gillingham on September 29, 1973 – even on the right wing. Story of my football life that. Setters was the first to play me out wide – Cloughie was another – but I never really enjoyed it.

It's not easy being a winger. You can't do right for doing wrong. Not seeing anything of the ball, you come inside to try to get involved. That gets you a bollocking from managers for not holding your right position. Stay wide for 90 minutes without getting a kick and your bollocking is for not getting back enough to help the team out.

I always saw myself as a striker roaming across the front line. I was never a centre forward, however many times Big Jack Charlton played me there at Wednesday. I told him 'how do you expect me to win the ball in the air against a defender who is 6'4""?' But he was always right and I was always wrong. That was another lesson that I soon learnt about professional football.

That day in Kent I didn't care where I played. Our goalkeeper saw most of the action as the Gills took us to the cleaners 5-1. I thought that I did ok but remember the roasting the manager gave us afterwards. Welcome to the Football League, Terry!

I say Terry but that isn't my real name. There is a 'Terry' in the Curran family but I'm Edward or 'Teddy'. But once Johnny Quigley, Donny's assistant manager, put my name out as Terry, it got into the press and it stuck. The rest of me is real enough, even the hair. Everyone thought that I permed it whilst I was playing, but it was 100 per cent natural – and still is!

There weren't too many highlights for Donny during my 14 months there, but an FA Cup tie with mighty Liverpool stands out. Here's a difference between football today and back in 1973. Teams in Donny's position now aren't bothered about the FA Cup. They give squad players a game, park the bus and hope not to lose 10 nil. That's why this fantastic competition is just a shadow of what it used to be. Liverpool's Jurgen Klopp picked a youth team in the 2019/20 competition, beating Everton 1-0 with players nowhere near his Premier League squad. When Shrewsbury, roughly comparable to Donny, played at Anfield in the next round, Klopp didn't even turn up.

Back then, Bill Shankly picked all of his superstars, despite Liverpool being top of the First Division and Donny, bottom of Division Four, did the same. I wasn't a sub. too many times in my career but was pleased to be on the bench that freezing afternoon.

What a match that was! It took a skinny young Donny lad called Kevin Keegan to stop his home club from winning. You know him, that other guy who did have permed hair. Keegan was getting his feet under the table following his transfer from Scunthorpe United and saved Liverpool with a couple of goals.

Peter Kitchen cancelled out the first and big Brendan O'Callaghan had us in dream land when he put us 2-1 in front by half time. Setters had to bring the lads down from the ceiling in the Anfield dressing room. He knew that the second half would be long and difficult.

Keegan quickly made it 2-2 and we were under pressure. Amazingly we nearly won it with a couple of minutes to go when Kitchen lobbed the ball over England goalkeeper Ray Clemence. The ball bounced back off the bar only for Emlyn 'crazy horse' Hughes to slice it back against the woodwork again and over. We were that close! The Liverpool fans gave us a great reception at the end – that's never changed. They've always been among the most sporting fans when the opposition has done well.

The replay was even more memorable because this time I started. An incredible 22,000 fans filled every inch of Belle Vue on a Tuesday afternoon during Edward Heath's three-day week. Liverpool full back Alec Lindsay, one of the game's hard men, told me that he'd break my leg if I went near him. I gave it him straight back and took a knock instead from Ray Clemence when I bounced off him after he beat me to a ball. I realised that I wasn't going to get it and put my shoulder into him. He turned around full on and I hit his shoulder – and flew back five or six yards. That taught me another lesson. I needed to work in the gym to become physically strong enough to play against men who knew all the tricks of the trade.

Liverpool won 2-0 and went on to lift the FA Cup, silencing Newcastle United's Super Mac, Malcolm MacDonald, who told the world what he was going to do in the final and barely got a kick as they were beaten 3-0. We improved too, finishing third from bottom!

My first goal in professional football came a couple of months later in a Yorkshire derby win over Rotherham United. I'd like to say that I beat half-a-dozen defenders and bent one into the top corner from 25 yards, But to be honest, I can't remember too much about it!

I suffered a strange injury when I broke the smallest bone in my body, the scaphoid. It happened when I fell in a reserve game and landed on my thumb. The pain was terrible and I had to go to hospital where a pot was put on my arm. I was told to wear it for six months, but it only lasted three days because Setters wanted me to play for the first team on the Saturday. Off came the pot and I played in the match. The hospital refused to see me again when they heard what I had done and this has resulted in damage to my thumb that I live with today.

We weren't much better in my second season. We scored a few goals, which was good for me, but let in a lot more. When we scored four at Shrewsbury's Gay Meadow, they got seven! The owners weren't happy and I suffered the sad sight of Setters departing in tears. Luckily his replacement Stan Anderson was even better to me.

I can laugh now at some of those memories, but there were some good footballers in that Donny team. I'm still in touch with

Peter Kitchen, a very good technical player who scored bags of goals for Donny and became a legend at Orient. Kitch wasn't always first choice during my spell at Belle Vue, but I didn't know why. He and big Brendan O'Callaghan, a more traditional type of centre forward, made a good strike partnership.

I shared digs with Brendan, one of my first mates in football. A clever man who had more O-levels to his name than Donny won matches in a season, he looked after me when I got into trouble and put up with my night clubbing. I found it hard to come down after matches and went to a night club and an all-night coffee bar on Saturdays, getting in between 5am and 6am before politely turning down Brendan's offer to go to Mass. He was a good Catholic, Brendan, and a good player.

When you think we had Mickey Elwiss and me on the flanks, it's a surprise we didn't blow away a few more teams. Problem was we never gave our own goalkeeper much protection. It was nice to hear news recently of Kim Book, brother of former Manchester City legend Tony, who had one of the most difficult jobs in football. Back then, I was more interested in reminding him of when he kept goal for Northampton when Bestie hit him for six.

Well-known managers took interest in me, including the great Bobby Charlton when he was at Preston. He had come to watch Elwiss against Stockport County at Edgeley Park. I was on the edge of their penalty area when we threw a lot of players forward for a late corner. Their centre half headed the ball powerfully forward which left their striker one-on-one with our defender Stan Brookes. I realised what was going to happen and chased back about 50 yards to make a saving tackle.

Charlton was in the players' lounge afterwards and said what I'd done was 'remarkable'. He'd come to scout Elwiss and was keen to sign me as well – but soon I was on my way to join another famous manager!

I played 75 games for Donny, scored 11 goals and laid on a fair few. Me and Donny was a win-win. I didn't stay long but they got me for nowt, paid me £2,000 in wages and sold me in a £75,000 deal to Nottingham Forest.

They needed the cash; I needed the chance to progress. They also got two very useful players from Forest in part exchange in goalkeeper, Dennis Peacock, and winger, Ian Miller, which may have helped to swing the deal with Donny when other clubs were in the frame.

My two seasons on Trentside under the great Brian Clough changed my football life and set me up for what should have been a long career in the topflight. I should have stayed longer at Nottingham Forest and been a bigger part of their amazing success story.

The first season saw me settling in at the club. Most of the lads who went to win European Cup medals were already there when I signed including John Robertson, Tony Woodcock, Ian Bowyer, Viv Anderson, John McGovern, Martin O'Neill and Frank Clark.

I was quite isolated during my first few months. It didn't help that I was taking Martin's place. I felt that the likes of Martin, Robbo, Viv, Jimmy McCann and Glyn Saunders made things difficult for me. I wasn't really welcomed into the club or invited to have a coffee with the lads.

I had another setback when I suffered a strange illness during the early winter after taking a flu jab. I was staying in digs and woke in the middle of the night feeling very unwell. I felt red hot inside, but my body was freezing. So I grabbed some Ralgex and rubbed that in and felt like I was on fire.

I went into training the next morning and still wasn't feeling well. One or two of the lads were taking the mickey, as they do, particularly when I told them about the Ralgex. When I went to see the club doctor, he asked me what I had eaten. I told him nothing unusual, but I had had the flu jab the day before. From there, I was sent to Harlow Wood Hospital where I spent the next week or so.

When my parents visited me, I was a real mess. I was on tubes, some of my hair was falling out, my skin was peeling, I was losing the nails on my fingers and toes and I couldn't even lift my head up. The dermatologist was also confused about what had happened. At first, he said he thought it was the result of a dirty needle, then he went back on that and talked about whether I'd had an allergic reaction to the flu jab. I'll never know for sure if that was the cause but that was the last time I took the injection. Footballers are given it routinely every winter, but I kept away from it. Forest kept the illness away from the media, who must have thought that I had a slight injury, and thankfully I was soon feeling better. The experience did, however, teach me one thing – never to have the flu jab.

I was out for a couple of months before returning to score my first Forest goal from the penalty spot in a 4-0 home victory over Carlisle. A lot of fans probably don't realise that it was me who had the spot kick duties at that stage ahead of Robbo who went on to score so many important penalties for the club.

The turning point for me as regards being accepted was a midweek friendly that we played at Corby Town. We sat in the communal bath afterwards and Robbo, who everyone looked up to, turned to me and said: "You can play football." I made some comments back about how I felt they had taken the piss out of me but, from that moment, I was one of the lads.

I also learnt a very important lesson from that season – it takes time to turn a football club around, even with a manager as brilliant as Cloughie in charge. We were very average for most of the 1975/76 season before we showed some glimpses of what we were capable of towards the end. We finished eighth, well outside the promotion race, after winning our last eight City Ground matches.

We all expected better things during the following campaign which soon saw Clough joined by his old sparring partner, Peter Taylor. That season saw me produce some of the best football of my career, although things started quietly enough with just three points from our first four games.

We were then 2-0 down at home to newly promoted Hereford before Ian Bowyer inspired a comeback that saw us win 4-3. That was the start of a run of City Ground games that Forest fans remember to this day with Carlisle conceding five, Jimmy Sirrel's Sheffield United being hit for six, then five more against Burnley.

It's probably difficult for Forest fans to imagine that John Robertson used to complain that he wasn't seeing enough of the ball because most of it was being directed down my flank. That was one of the reasons why Robbo wasn't keen on playing on the left wing in the first place. Instead he fancied himself as a central midfield player where he could be more involved. The problem was that nobody else did. Robbo never had the physical fitness to get around the pitch and it was a total masterstroke when Clough and Taylor swapped him with Ian Bowyer, who'd been playing wide left. It was mostly after I'd gone that Forest switched their direction of play to the other flank where Frank Clark had one main job – give Robbo the ball!

I was electric in those City Ground games, having the freedom to run at defenders and cause all sorts of panic in the opposition's defence. There were times when I was so quick that I ran off and back onto the pitch to get beyond the full back. The local media loved it and I was being considered for the first time for England Under 23s.

Just before I was injured, Cloughie pulled me up in training and spoke about playing me up front or in midfield. Like most clubs, we tended to play eight or nine-a-side games in training with individuals occupying different positions. He thought that, because I was very physically fit, I could do a job in the middle of the park, but I was keener on his idea of playing me further forward. I honestly think that would have happened at some stage had I not been badly injured.

When Forest were in town, word was that I was the man to stop and that meant I got some rough treatment. But the injury which did stop me was a total accident. McGovern played a hospital pass and Paul Fletcher caught me on the knee as I went for the ball. I collapsed in a heap but at first there was no pain. It then became clear that the knee had locked and I went to hospital for an x-ray where they discovered that I'd damaged my cruciate ligaments.

I was in plaster for six weeks, in hospital for two months and out of the side for about four. I still look back and wonder what I would have achieved at Forest had that not happened when it did.

I was desperate to get back onto the pitch and help the club with their promotion push. It was a very up and down campaign which looked for a long time as if we might pull up just short.

Eventually, the boss asked on a Friday how I was feeling and I told him that I was ready to play. He called me in for a one-to-one with him on the Sunday and I expected he was going to do some training with me. I was very disappointed when Clough ordered me to do 20 laps round the pitch but did what I was told. Next day I was back in training with the first team.

My first game back was a midweek visit to struggling Hereford United. We hadn't won a game for more than a month and needed a lift. It wasn't the greatest of matches, but I felt it went well because we won 1-0 and I scored the only goal. I was then very angry when Peter Taylor accused me of being a coward, saying that I'd pulled back from a couple of tackles. Anyone would have been forgiven for being a bit cautious after the seriousness of my injury, but I wasn't that kind of player. I was very brave and never gave an inch.

I kept my place for the trip to Carlisle United on the Saturday which ended in frustration. We took the lead late on, but allowed Carlisle to equalise before I set up a last second chance for Tony Woodcock that I'm still not sure how he missed. Little did I realise that was going to be my last contribution as a first team player at Forest.

I was looking forward to the derby game with Notts County at the City Ground and furious when Clough told me I needed a rest. Rest? I'd done nothing but rest for the last few months and was desperate to play. Cloughie told me that because my injury had been so bad – it was very similar to the one that ended his own playing career. When I say the manager's door came off its hinges when I stormed out of his office, people may think I'm exaggerating. But it honestly did and Cloughie sat there laughing his head off.

I was then on the sidelines as the lads finished the season with a nervy 1-0 home win over Millwall. It could never happen these days but our rivals for the third and final promotion spot, Bolton, still had three matches to play and needed five more points to deny us.

The nerves jangled still further when they beat Cardiff, but we got the break that we needed the following weekend when Bolton were somehow beaten 1-0 on their own patch by champions Wolves, whose goalkeeper was carried off injured in the first half.

We celebrated promotion on the plane to Spain for our end-of-season holiday and I was looking forward to First Division football with Brian Clough.

All went well on our pre-season tour of Germany and with Kenny Burns being our only confirmed new signing, I was expecting to be in the side for the big kick off against Everton at Goodison Park. Instead, Cloughie went for the more conservative option of playing my mate, Martin O'Neill, in a more withdrawn wide role with the great John Robertson on the other flank.

It all came to a head in a very funny way a week later after I'd again been left out of the side to play Derby. I went into the manager's office on the Monday morning expecting to see Cloughie face to face and tell him for a third time that I wanted a transfer. This time I was so serious that I had a letter with me in the inside of my coat pocket.

I was taken off guard though because only Peter Taylor was in there. He told me that Brian was having a day off and asked whether he could help. I said no because I wanted to speak with the organ grinder, rather than the monkey, and walked back out of the office.

Then I changed my mind, charged back into the room without knocking on the door and threw a piece of paper on the desk telling Taylor to give it to the boss. After I'd walked back out into the car park, I saw Taylor running after me shouting, "What do you want me to do with this?"

This made me even more angry because he was trying to hand the paper back to me. I ignored Pete and got into the car, only for him to knock on the car window and shout again. I opened the car window and said, "Give it to the boss."

He said, "It's your electric bill". So I reached into my coat and got out the other letter which contained my transfer request and handed that to Taylor.

"So what do you want me to do with the electric bill?"

"Give it to the boss and tell him to pay it!" I replied. And he did. If you think I'm kidding, ask any of the other Forest lads.

Cloughie played me at my own game. I asked if any clubs had been in for me, after I'd been privately tapped up by Derby County, and he said 'only Bury, they want to take you on loan'. "I'll go there then," I said and he was shocked.

I went to Bury about a week later. I decided to stay in Lancashire, rather than travel daily from Nottingham and was put up in a bed and breakfast near their Gigg Lane ground. I played two or three games in a side, including future Wednesday manager Danny Wilson, and Keith Kennedy, brother of Liverpool's Alan.

Then I took a call from Clough at the bed and breakfast in which he said 'who said you could train there? I said you could go on loan, but you train here." I said I would see Bury manager Bobby Smith and talk it through with him.

We were at the ground when Bobby phoned Cloughie who denied speaking with me at all! I only played one more game before returning to Forest before the end of my month's loan.

I could still have saved my relationship with Forest and Clough, even after my former teammate, John Middleton, sounded me out about a move down the A52 to Derby to play for Tommy Docherty. John explained how keen the Doc was on signing me and said I should demand a move.

Even when I was halfway out of the door, Clough promised to tear the contract up and was happy for me to stay at Forest. There was a tear in his eye at the end. Leaving the City Ground when I did was one of my biggest mistakes in football – if not the biggest – but that's not how I saw it back then.

All my football life I wanted to play – as simple as that. I could never have been like today's players seeing out their contracts on big wages. Call me what you like – naïve, arrogant - I am what I am. So I left Forest to play first team football with Derby County.

CHAPTER TWO

THE DOC AND THE SAINTS

What Southampton manager LAWRIE McMENEMY really thought about Terry Curran.

Speaking as a TV pundit, he said: "There is no doubt in my mind that given greater consistency Curran would have been a regular member of the England team.

"In addition to his pace, Curran can always be relied upon to do the unexpected.

"I was once discussing this aspect of Curran's game with Ron Atkinson and Ron, recalling his days at West Bromwich Albion, said that his full back Derek Statham reported that Curran was the winger he least liked to play against because he never knew what he was going to do."

*****

YOU may be surprised when I say that Derby County were the best team that I played for, but they honestly were. Their potential, when you look at the players at the Baseball Ground, was almost limitless. Considering they had won the First Division title twice inside four seasons and appointed one of the era's iconic managers in Tommy Docherty, they looked set for more success. In my mind I was taking a step up moving from Forest to Derby.

The Rams rather than Forest had household names in their side. Roy McFarland and Colin Todd were fantastic, classy defenders who brought the ball out from the back with style and confidence. Gerry Daly, Don Masson and Bruce Rioch were top midfielders and they had the best striker in the country, in my opinion, in Charlie George.

They were so good there were times I found myself watching what my teammates were doing in training rather than concentrating on my game. Playing with Charlie George, one of my idols, was a big shock. And again he lived up to what I thought of him – a good man and gentle character who said what was on his mind and would do anything he could for you. We all learn from the top players and that was what I did at the Baseball Ground.

Yet the success I expected never happened. The Rams finished 12th in the season that I played for them, whilst Forest were champions. It could so easily have been the other way around.

The serious talent in that squad rarely produced the very best performances on the pitch. Our highlight was an midweek night under the lights at the Baseball Ground when we played Liverpool off the park. We beat a side who were still a major force and shortly to win the European Cup 4-2.. That form would have been made us title contenders, but instead was a one-off.

I liked and got on well with Tommy Doc, but some of my teammates thought he was a liar. To be honest, managers sometimes tell players 'white lies' because they can't please everyone and that was Doc, in my view. I don't think Doc's mind was fully on the job after what happened at Manchester United. That club was his love. Not only had he lost his 'dream job' at Old Trafford, the fallout from his affair with Mary Brown, wife of the club's physiotherapist, was still raw. Taking the sort of abuse opposition fans dished out home and away every Saturday – with chants of 'who's up Mary Brown? - would have an affect on anyone and Tommy Doc was no different.

A wheeler dealer in the transfer market, The Doc liked to buy and sell players for whatever reason. I'll leave you to read between the lines and apply your common sense.

Doc was almost as big a hit with the media as Cloughie with his cheeky, quick humour. Anyone who heard him at a speakers' evening in later years will tell you he was as funny and witty as anyone. The difference with Clough was he lacked the trophies and success to back it up. He chopped and changed looking for a winning side and never had the same bond with his players.

In my opinion, had Derby been managed by a Clough or a Bob Paisley, they could have challenged for the league title and the major cup competitions. Only recently I chatted with Don Masson and he said much the same thing.

No disrespect to Forest and how great some of their players turned out to be, the main difference between the two sides was Clough, who pulled off masterstrokes playing Robbo wide on the left and signing one of the best goalkeepers in the world in Peter Shilton. Having a goalkeeper of that status wins you major trophies. I was a friend of John Middleton, who sadly passed away a few years ago, and I'm not having a go at him..

Card schools involving the club's top names were legendary whilst I was at the Baseball Ground including a very merry Christmas, when Charlie George, Colin Todd, Billy Hughes and Gerry Daly and co. partied into the early hours before a game against Ipswich. Wine, beer and £1,600 in the card pot, playing chase the ace, wasn't the perfect preparation for an important game, but star quality shone through. Charlie scored one of his specials as we returned home with the points and The Doc none the wiser over what happened in the hotel room. Either he didn't know what was going on or wasn't bothered.

Derby was a great place to play football. The facilities at the club were second only to Everton in my playing career. There was always a great atmosphere at the old Baseball Ground with the fans being very close. Unfortunately the pitch was either very boggy or full of sand. That didn't help us play the good football we were capable of.

The club still hadn't got over the Clough and Taylor controversy, despite winning a title under Dave Mackay. They had both been very popular and I could still sense the disappointment from chairman Sam Longson turning against Clough who told me Longson encouraged him to do his TV broadcasts then tried everything to reign him back in.

I achieved one of my dreams by playing at Old Trafford for the first time in my career in the January, but it wasn't a happy return for The Doc as we got well beaten 4-0.

I felt I did reasonably well without hitting the heights I had at Forest. When a player returns from a serious injury, it takes a while to get back to peak fitness. I had a good game against Forest at the Baseball Ground in February in a 0-0 draw but by that time Clough and co were well on the way to glory and we were playing for pride.

Match of the Day cameras saw me score my first ever goal in the topflight - a consolation in the 3-1 defeat to Birmingham City – and I netted again in what proved to be my last game, a 3-0 win over Arsenal. The positive way that we ended the season – also including a 4-1 win over relegated Leicester City – meant that I had no reason to think my stay would be so short.

Events then took a surprise turn when a reporter phoned to tell me Lawrie McMenemy at Southampton was interested in signing me. Doc's attitude when I spoke with him disappointed me. I thought I was in his future plans but instead he said: "If you want to go, go." When a manager says something like that, you know they're not desperate to keep you. That made my decision easy.

So, in a hectic 12 months, I went to a third First Division club. McMenemy had been looking for a winger and I understand striker Ted MacDougall recommended me as a player with a bright future.

McMenemy was also one of the most respected and highest profile managers of his time, having led Saints to promotion after pulling off an FA Cup shock when beating Manchester United at Wembley in 1976.

McMenemy was liked by the media and highly rated by the suits at the FA. He is widely regarded as a Saints legend for his long spell on the south coast and that's fair play. With the possible exception of Ted Bates, he was probably the most successful manager in the club's history. It was a major achievement to lead Saints to second finish in the First Division in 1984 and he brought big stars to The Dell including Kevin Keegan and Peter Shilton.

The McMenemy I knew treated the more experienced players a lot better than the younger ones. I never let him do that with me. I stood up to McMenemy, meaning there were plenty of ups and downs.

Saints played good football under McMenemy but were also street-wise. Sometimes he singled out an opposition player such as Tony Currie who had some very good games against us. McMenemy's teams weren't recognised by the pundits as being particularly hard but had players who could take care of themselves. He told two or three different players to kick the opposition's star man so they would get away without getting booked. It was thought back then every player had a 'free' tackle or two.

Both McMenemy and I have had our say about each other in public – but there's no lack of respect on either side.

McMenemy wrote that he didn't like my attitude and wanted me 'out of the club by Christmas'. But I know the truth. We had our differences as people but, like all the other managers I played for, McMenemy rated me. That's why he offered me a three-year contract at Saints and made it as difficult as possible for me to leave. Then, of course, he signed me for Sunderland years later.

My happiest times at The Dell were mostly with Alan Ball. For some reason we clicked as mates from the time we met,even though we were at very different stages of our careers. I walked into the dressing room wearing a short leather Christian Dior jacket worth £400 and light blue jeans and Bally quipped: "Where's your motorbike?" "It's outside," I replied. He liked that.

We were friends from that moment – the established star, World Cup and First Division title winning player and the brash young man still making his way in the game. I'm not sure McMenemy appreciated it though. Bally had been a sounding board for the manager, now he was spending more time with me.

After signing for Saints, I sorted a few things out in Derby before returning to my lonely hotel. Bally knew how I'd be feeling so popped along to welcome me to the club. There we talked about football, including Bally's experience in winning the World Cup. I found out that he came from a similar background and, like me, loved his Dad who kept his feet on the ground however well he did. Bally was a true Englishman, very proud to have played for his country and extra proud to have won the World Cup.

His football didn't suffer in the last stages of his career because he was such a good technical player. Being a midfield player is about making the right decisions and Bally made them practically all the time. When he got caught in possession, it was usually because he'd been given a bad pass. Unlike many footballers from my era, Bally would have lapped up the modern day game. He'd have been the perfect fit in Barcelona's midfield when they were passing the ball for fun and dominating European competition.

In my opinion Alan Ball ran Southampton whilst I was there – and I got in bad books with McMenemy for telling him so. Put it this way, I never asked the manager who was in the team – Bally always knew.

I found Bally the perfect mix – a world class footballer who liked to socialise. Bally gave talks to prisoners about what they were missing out on the outside and privately compared prison and the life of a footballer.

He explained this after a great night in Marbella. We had been in Sean Connery's bar and Bally was a bit worse for wear when we got back to our hotel room at about 3.15am. Lights were off and we were in our beds but after five minutes Bally, still wide awake, said: "this is like being in prison." I asked what he meant as we were in a beautiful place enjoying ourselves. He said we had been ordered to be back in by a certain time and that's what he meant by being in prison. So we got back up and had another hour out!

We were due up for 7am to play golf - Bally made it, I didn't. It wasn't the drink; I wasn't feeling well. It didn't do us any harm as, after flying back home on the Thursday and having a light training session, we beat Manchester City 2-1 on the Saturday at Maine Road.

After our night out at Cinderella Rockefella in Leeds, we were in the bath in the hotel room early in the morning when he again started talking. Bally was thinking ahead to another night in a hotel in Blackpool where we were staying ahead of the weekend's FA Cup tie at Preston. He said any night spent in a hotel with fellow footballers was like being inside. It was snowing and Bally was already convinced the Blackpool match would be called off, so made plans to visit his friend Brian London's night club. The night worked out perfectly. Bally made his escape from the hotel via the drainpipe and, luckily, the FA Cup tie was postponed.

Bally often rang me on our day off to arrange an afternoon or evening out. We were both married, so he made an excuse such as we had been asked to present some football awards. Instead we went horse racing to Salisbury, Fontwell, Newbury, Sandown or Ascot then on to bars and night clubs for a few drinks.

Bally, bless him, was a great help to me at Southampton. We kept in touch after he retired from playing and he invited me back to Blackpool when he was manager there to look at his team training. Like a lot of superstars, he found it difficult coaching at a lower level. He and others couldn't understand why players found it difficult to control and pass a ball. The only way he could have developed a team to play his way would have been to find young, gifted lads on the way up or skilled players coming towards the end of their careers.

Bally wasn't the only superstar at Saints - Charlie George was as big a presence after joining from Derby. Altogether we were a good side with strong players in all the key positions from Terry Gennoe in goal, Chris Nicholl and Malcolm Waldron at centre back, full backs Ivan Golac and David Peach, Bally, Steve Williams, Nick Holmes in the middle of the park and natural goalscorers Ted MacDougall and Phil Boyer up front. A few players short of challenging for the title maybe, but well worth Bally's £25 bets on us to win the League Cup and the FA Cup.

I remember giving Wolves full back Geoff Palmer a roasting in a man of the match performance as we won 3-2 win at The Dell, and had a particularly good game when we thrashed Everton 3-0. But our season really started to take shape when we beat Manchester City 2-1 to reach the semi finals of the League Cup and West Brom by the same scoreline to get into the last eight of the FA Cup.

The West Brom game later caused friction between me and McMenemy. He was on the pitch giving a team talk before the start of extra time. I tried to attract his attention and he ignored me until I told him I was bursting to go to the toilet. I feel McMenemy belittled me in his book when I was only trying to be respectful whilst he was making tactical points and not just run off the pitch..

These days the League Cup has lost its importance but for us it meant everything. We were just a two-legged semi-final away from playing at Wembley which was a big personal ambition of mine. No way would we have thought about putting out below strength sides in a competition that we could win.

I will always be remembered at Saints for scoring the goal that took us to the Twin Towers, my only goal for the club. We snatched a 2-2 draw from the first leg, despite being outplayed throughout the whole match at Elland Road and it was a much tighter game at The Dell. Sometimes you need to think on your feet to score and this happened after a good move involving Bally, Nick Holmes

Getting my first taste
of First Division
football with Derby.

Tommy Docherty didn't get the best out of Derby's star studded side.

My winning goal against Leeds took the Saints to Wembley.

Big Jack Charlton signed me for Sheffield Wednesday.

There was no better feeling than scoring for Wednesday.

Defenders tried anything to stop me getting past them!

Tony Kenworthy was in my shadow in the Sheffield derby.

Celebrating promotion after a 0-0 draw against Carlisle.

A piece of play acting from Simon Stainrod led to a red card for
me - and a riot!

Hillsborough houses some of the country's most loyal fans.

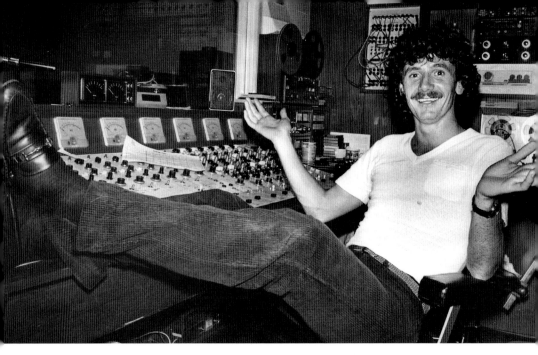

My version of 'Singing the Blues' is still played at
Hillsborough today.

Luton feel the pain as I net at Hillsorough.

**I formed a goal scoring partnership with Andy
McCulloch at the Owls.**

Never a Blade, but I gave my all when at Bramall Lane.

I was a flying winger, but it wasn't my best position.

Enjoying my first taste of European club action with Everton.

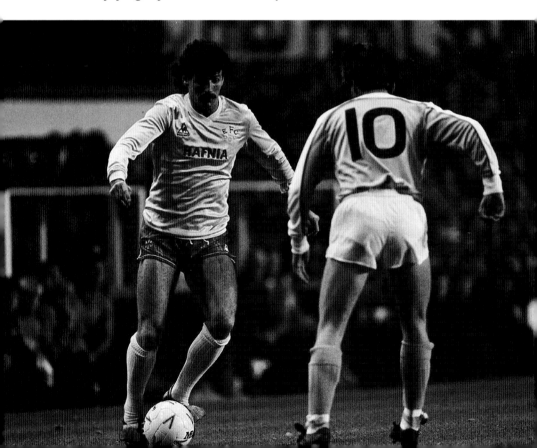

and Trevor Hebberd. I was in the perfect place when he crossed but the ball took a nick off full back Frank Gray and bounced up awkwardly, making it look like I had miscontrolled it. But quick thinking helped me to get a shot off which flew high past Scottish international goalkeeper David Harvey.

I'd already been approached by Jack Charlton to join Sheffield Wednesday, but stayed at The Dell to make my one and only Wembley appearance in the final against my old club Forest when we lost a memorable match 3-2. That was so nearly the perfect day for me – I was playing football at Wembley alongside my great mate, Alan Ball, against Brian Clough, the manager who I rated as number one and afterwards Bally and I met up with my other idol George Best at Tramps night club in London. The only missing piece was the result, although for more than half the game that looked like going my way too.

I approached the final with a lot on my mind. Here I was fulfilling one of my ambitions by playing at the national stadium and the most important aim in my mind was to get one over on Brian Clough. It wasn't that I wanted revenge for how things ended for me at Forest but that was a sign of the huge respect I had for the manager.

McMenemy told me as we went out onto the turf for a look round that 'this is your chance to show Brian Clough what you can do – you can be our matchwinner today' but I already knew that. I was already weighing up my dual with Frank Clark, the experienced former Newcastle United full back and how I could get the better of him.

I respected all my opponents and Frank was different from many I faced. He wasn't the kind to give his man verbal abuse but read the game particularly well and was very good at covering and intercepting rather than kicking players up in the air like many full backs. He was also unusual as a left back as he was naturally right footed.

McMenemy's first battle had been to try to keep me out of reach of Clough and my former Forest teammates – but that tussle had already been lost. As soon as we went into the tunnel, Cloughie was there saying: "Young man, good luck today but you're not going to have a good game because Frank Clark will be all over you."

Knowing that I'd soon be on my way to Sheffield Wednesday was never going to distract me from the job in hand. Anyone will tell you that as soon as you get onto the pitch, everything else in your life is forgotten for the next 90 minutes.

Folklore has it that the reason Forest started so slowly was that Cloughie had encouraged them to stay up drinking in their hotel the night before. It's a good story which always gets a lot of laughs on the after dinner speaking circuit. There were tales of players being told to come down from their hotel room late at night to join in the drinking session and one or two having to be carried upstairs afterwards because they were in such a bad state. Then they were still coming round whilst we were dominating much of the first half before, having sobered up completely, they put us to the sword after half time.

Like so many of those stories, however, it just wasn't true. I played under Brian Clough and kept in contact with some of the lads and know he wouldn't have allowed them to behave like that. Cloughie was happy for the team to have one or two drinks to relax them the night before the game but not to go over the top and get drunk.

Instead, it was our good play that forced Forest onto the back foot, even before a great through ball from Bally gave left back David Peach the chance to take the ball round Peter Shilton and give us a 17th minute lead.

The rest of the half was also ours and we had one or two good chances to increase our lead. I was having a good battle with Clark on the right flank. I think it is fair to say that we both played well. Only towards the end of the half did Forest start to come back into the tie.

McMenemy warned us that Cloughie would have them firing in the second half and, of course, I didn't need telling. But from the kick off the game took a different direction. We needed to see off Forest's initial flurry of attacks and there was one moment that I will always remember.

Forest had just gone close and forced a corner when the ball broke to me midway through our half. This was a rare chance for me to really stretch my legs and I outpaced a couple of Forest players to take the ball to the edge of their penalty area. I should perhaps have laid the ball inside with Forest stretched but the ball bounced awkwardly and, with half a shout for a foul, the chance was lost.

Had we gone 2-0 up at that stage I'm convinced that we would have gone home with the cup. Instead, we were soon back to 1-1 having played a large part in our own downfall. The normally reliable Nick Holmes gave the ball away to John Robertson, then a fatal misunderstanding between Chris Nicholl and Terry Gennoe allowed Garry Birtles to nip in for the equaliser. Shortly after that Birtles outpaced Nicholl to shoot Forest 2-1 up and suddenly we were up against it.

Forest were now full of confidence and looked to be out of sight when Archie Gemmill slipped Tony Woodcock through to make it 3-1 but still we didn't give up. Holmes fired a snap shot past Shilton with a few minutes left and Shilts made one more save to prevent us getting an equaliser.

Overall Forest deserved their win, but we knew we had our chances. I have watched the game back several times since and, looking at it with the eyes of a coach, we could have won. We had the clearer opportunities to score in the first half whilst they were limited to half chances, then we shot ourselves in the foot over a 20-minute spell. Forest fans will say they forced us into mistakes but, in my view, it was our errors rather than their brilliant play that turned the tie.

I was turning in very good performances for Saints and could easily have stayed longer but for two obstacles – my relationship with McMenemy and the fact that the club who wanted me most was Sheffield Wednesday.

McMenemy and Saints tried to the very last to frustrate me to see if they could change my mind. I had been to the races at Newbury with Bally when my wife told me that McMenemy had phoned. I told him straight that I didn't like him and wanted to leave.

Even on transfer deadline day, they were playing mind games with me. I was due to go to FA headquarters in central London with Lou Chatterley, McMenemy's assistant, to sign the forms. It's a fair journey from Southampton and, even then, getting through the capital was a nightmare, yet Lou left it as late as possible to set off in his car. We were crawling through London when I told Lou to stop the car and I hailed a black taxi to try to get there in time. Luckily I did so, with Lou arriving a few minutes later. I think they were hoping that we would fail to meet the deadline so that I couldn't play for Wednesday in the remaining games of that season and then they might be able to persuade me to continue playing for Saints.

Looking back on it all these years later, we probably both needed our heads knocking together. I would have been good for McMenemy and having longer at Southampton would have been good for me. But we make our decisions at the time and live with them.

McMenemy put his spin on my departure to spare his blushes. He wrote that I preferred to be a 'bigger fish in a small pond' rather than test my skills at a higher level. He can think what he likes. It must have been embarrassing for him to lose a player to a Third Division club, so he did his best to explain it to Saints fans.

CHAPTER THREE
SINGING THE BLUES AT HILLSBOROUGH

Sheffield Wednesday manager Jack Charlton speaking on Match of the Day in 1980.

"I would say Terry Curran is the most exciting player in English football at the moment – no question. He can be frustrating but then set the whole place alight in a second.

If you ask other managers who have managed Terry Curran, they will say he is a funny kind of lad to handle, but not one of them has ever disagreed with his ability.

He has an in-built ability to take people on, he has got pace, he has got aggression and he can't understand why he has not played for England and I can't understand why he has not been near playing for England.

In this day and age of systems, you have got to have someone who can unlock the door, someone like him who has got the pace to attack people, go either side and finish and score goals and shift himself across the front line and not be picked up. You have got a player who is worthy to have played in that England team.

I keep saying to Terry 'Ay, you will get in. If we win 10 games in a row, people will start saying 'yes, he has got a bit of merit' because you tell me a more outstanding player in the Football League?"

*****

By STEVE ELLIS, Sheffield Wednesday club photographer since the 1970s.

THE JACK Charlton and Terry Curran era was my favourite time covering Sheffield Wednesday. It's fair to say Owls hadn't seen footballers like Terry before – he ranks in my top five best Wednesday players.

He had pace and power and did things other footballers never dreamt of. His relationship with Big Jack was love-hate because they were two people who were never wrong. I don't think I ever heard Jack admit he made a mistake, but he was a great bloke.

Those were far different times when the press socialised with the players. They had steak pie and chips and apple pie and custard in the café and we stayed up until 3am or 4am having a drink with Big Jack on away trips. It was good fun and we enjoyed our football.

Terry was one of the players I got to know. He asked me once to take his greyhound to Whitwood for him. His dog was in the fourth race but every time he heard the gun, he thought he was racing. When he raced for real, he was knackered on the final lap!

On the field, there were great memories. Hillsborough on Boxing Day stands out but, for me, Terry's goal at Bramall Lane was even better – one of the best I've ever seen. Promotion after the Carlisle game at Hillsborough was special, too, and it's a shame Jack's team faded away before we reached the First Division.

Terry was very hyper, always on the go. He'd knock on my door about 7.30am wanting to take me and Ian Vickers, the Sheffield Star reporter, for breakfast – remember we'd been up until a few hours before! He would tell us with the enthusiasm of a 16-year-old what he was going to do to the opposition that day.

Jack was a one-off too. We were on the coach for a game in London one Saturday afternoon when he suddenly told the driver to stop and he got off. He told us he was going to watch a player in another game in the city and to pick him up afterwards When we saw him again, he didn't know how we had got on!

When we were preparing for the FA Cup semi final against Brighton, I went with Maurice Setters to see captain Mike Lyons have a late fitness test at Hampstead Heath. When he got back to the hotel with the important news, Jack ignored us and continued reading his newspaper!

TC's a ticking time bomb in a way and we couldn't believe it when he signed for United. That made the front rather than the back pages in Sheffield. I lost touch with him for a while as I concentrated on Owls but it's great all these years later to still be a friend of one of my favourite players.

I've got a huge archive of Wednesday photos and have let Terry use a few of his choice in this book. They bring back memories of a player and a person who certainly did it his own way and will never be forgotten at Hillsborough.

*****

IMAGINE Jack Grealish, one of today's most talented players, quitting Premier League football and putting his hopes of playing for England on hold by signing for a League One club!

That's what I did when I left Southampton to join Wednesday. It would never happen today. Agents would go mad. But I was my own man and Wednesday are my club. My move was unusual back in 1979. Today's 24-hour football media would never stop talking about it.

I looked at it differently. Wednesday were two divisions below Southampton but were the bigger club. That's why Big Jack took the job as manager. Working alongside Big Jack as his number two was another man I had a lot of time for in Maurice Setters.

The job they took on was huge as Wednesday were rock bottom of the Third Division and in a total mess. It was some kind of success to scramble a mid-table finish during their first season at Hillsborough after suffering the embarrassment of being knocked out of the FA Cup by Wigan Athletic, then in the Northern Premier League.

Jack approached me trying to build a side capable of challenging for promotion. He thought the best way was a big, physically strong, team who were hard to beat. So he brought in 6'2" Andy McCulloch up front, replaced Chris Turner with big Bob Bolder between the sticks and signed Mike Pickering as a strong centre half.

I never fitted easily into the way Big Jack wanted to play. My football education came from Cloughie. He got Forest playing quick, passing football to feet. Ok, the centre backs lumped it every now and again rather than get caught in possession, but the manager told us: "If God wanted us to play in the sky, he'd have put grass there." He placed a football on a towel in the dressing room and told us to keep it there – on the floor. Derby and Saints weren't quite the same but played some football - Wednesday played none under Big Jack.

Wednesday showed their ambition by matching my £300 a week wages at Saints but my first few weeks were a culture shock. I had to be content with a place on the bench at Watford on the Saturday after my mad dash across London on transfer deadline day to sign. To make it worse we lost 1-0.

My Hillsborough debut was a big day for me. I looked forward all my life to playing for Wednesday in front of the type of passionate, large crowd that I was part of in the late 1960s. Instead there were only 11,065 people in the famous old ground as we got beat 2-1 by Mansfield Town.

Even that crowd looked big compared with the 4,200 spectators at Chester City where we scraped a 2-2 draw. Wednesday were an obvious target for opposition fans and players. We were the Third Division's version of Manchester United and everyone was up for playing us. I was even more of a marked man because I'd been in the First Division.

My first ever Wednesday goal came in a 1-1 draw at Boothferry Park against Hull City on Good Friday. It was a good Saturday, too, as 24 hours later Rodger Wylde scored twice as we beat local rivals Chesterfield 4-0. Yet the final three attendances at Hillsborough that season were all under five figures, including a miserable 7,310 to see us beat Blackpool.

A final position of 14th was modest but, at least, we weren't still flirting with relegation. Our highlight that season was an amazing FA Cup tie with Arsenal before I arrived which went to four replays. Imagine what the managers would say about that these days! In the end we lost 2-0 on a neutral ground at Leicester City's Filbert Street after getting much-needed attention from the national media for a few weeks. Another bonus at the end of the campaign was Sheffield United being relegated from Division Two, meaning the big Steel City derby was back.

The season started with all the usual hype and optimism, helped by a League Cup victory over Hull City with me getting a goal in the away leg. That was two goals for me at Boothferry Park and none at Hillsborough. I soon put that score right.

There was plenty of local rivalry to keep us on our toes as Barnsley, Chesterfield, Rotherham and Mansfield were also all in the same division.

The opening game of the season at Oakwell against Barnsley is one that fans still talk with me about. Amazingly, there were over 23,000 in the ground with the home supporters giving me plenty of stick. My haircut, appearance and manner always meant I got flack. They called me 'gypo' and a fair bit worse, but I didn't moan. It was part of the game, helping to create a good atmosphere. And it never put me off. I raised my game because I loved nothing more than sticking their words back down their throats.

My focus was on getting the better of Mick McCarthy, one of the hardest tacklers in the game. When players like him kicked me up in the air, I felt it, but never let them know how much. There was no rolling around on the ground pretending to be injured. We didn't want them to see they had got to us.

I will always remember getting our first league goal of that famous season and coming away with a 3-0 victory. But hopes of getting all the local bragging rights were soon ended when we lost 2-1 to a very good Chesterfield and McCarthy and co. got revenge by winning 2-0 at Hillsborough.

Heading a goal against Grimsby Town at Blundell Park was special. Big Jack knew that I could play on the ground but didn't rate me in the air, so bet £100 I wouldn't score with my head. I got myself in the penalty area like a good old-fashioned centre forward and rose above the goalkeeper to head home.

The first half of the campaign was up and down as we were sixth going into the famous Boxing Day game against leaders Sheffield United.

I never got too worked up before a game, but something was in the air that Christmas. Whether it was because the two Sheffield rivals hadn't played each other for a while, I don't know, but everyone in the city was talking about the match.

I'd enjoyed one of my best games in a Forest shirt in a 6-1 win over The Blades and I wanted it badly. None of us could have known though that Boxing Day 1979 was going to live in the memory of Owls fans for decades to come.

The City Council brought the kick off time forward to 11am and, being a Bank Holiday, there was no public transport. But nothing stopped fans packing into Hillsborough. The official attendance was 49,309, but you could add another 10,000 onto that. There'd never been anything like it for a Third Division game.

Folklore has it that we were all over The Blades from the kick off. It wasn't like that. The start was even until my mate Ian Mellor gave us a huge boost with a fantastic 25-yard shot. But United had their moments in the first half and could have been level. Bob Bolder's brilliant save and the woodwork ensured that we went in at the break with a 1-0 lead.

The second half was all Wednesday. We murdered them and I had one of my best games for the club. Many people remember me sliding on my knees in front of the Sheffield United fans to celebrate scoring our second goal. They thought I was goading their fans – but that wasn't the reason.

Scoring a goal is like nothing on earth, particularly in a big game in front of a crowd. What happens next is anybody's guess. I was lost in the moment, with no thought about anything other than the ball being in the back of the net. Ask any goalscorer, they'll tell you the same.

Big Jack enjoyed that one, but it cost him another £100 after I met Andy McCulloch's cross with a flying header. He should have believed me in the first place! I was pelted with coins by United fans behind the goal but didn't care about that either. We were 2-0 up and well on our way.

I could have got myself a second a few minutes later, but instead played in Jeff King for a close range finish. It's very rare that a side comes back from three goals down and we enjoyed ourselves after that. Running into the United penalty area, I was blatantly tripped by goalkeeper, Derek Richardson, and Mark Smith did what he did best from the spot to make it four.

That was like winning an FA Cup final to us. It gave us belief that we could pip Sheffield United for promotion. Of course, the game was special. Very few people remember our squeaky 1-0 wins that season, but all Wednesday fans of a certain age have stories about the Boxing Day massacre. At last count there must have been about 250,000 there!

I went to town off the field by getting myself an unofficial agent in Gerry Webster, forming a fan club and even releasing a single *Singing the Blues*. I was told of a way that it could have made *Top of the Pops* but wasn't interested in playing the system. It sold about 3,500 copies and I'm proud that it's still played regularly at Hillsborough to this day – a lasting reminder that I'm a Wednesdayite!

Life was great as we went on a 16-match unbeaten run to put us firmly in the hunt for promotion whilst Blades faded badly. This coincided with Big Jack putting me up front with big Andy McCulloch which suited us both fine. We were good mates off the field and combined well on it. I've said from day one that my best position was as a striker roaming across the front line but didn't play there enough. Andy's strength and battling qualities opened up chances for me to cash in with my pace. I banged in nine goals in just 12 games, the best goalscoring spell of my career. Andy wasn't far behind either as we smashed five past Bury and Rotherham, despite Big Jack's caution.

The Chesterfield and Rotherham derbies attracted more than 20,000 fans to Hillsborough showing that the Boxing Day gate wasn't such a one off. I always knew the fans would return if we started winning. Scoring a few goals made us better value for their hard-earned money.

Wimbledon's visit was one that I looked forward to for months – although not for footballing reasons. It all started after the away match at Plough Lane where I'd scored a couple of goals in our 4-3 win. What happened in the bar afterwards was even better.

Women looked at me – being a footballer helped, particularly after a good game! This time I was minding my own business getting a coke when I felt something in my back pocket. It was a piece of paper with the name of a woman and her telephone number. The message was to ring her when Wimbledon visited Hillsborough. As I looked around the room, a very sexy blonde mouthed 'I mean it' to me! I guarded that piece of paper with my life. I rang her a week later and we had a nice chat. She was the girlfriend or wife of one of the Wimbledon players. I told her to ring me back a few days before the game.

It wasn't difficult for her to pull this off without her bloke knowing because she knew he would be in Sheffield on the

Friday night with the rest of the Wimbledon team. She arranged for match tickets to be left for her at the ground, but instead of travelling north on the Saturday came a day early to meet me at Sheffield railway station.

I booked a room at the Rutland Hotel because it was nearby and fairly discreet. I also needed a pass out from my wife to make it work. She knew the team sometimes stayed together overnight before away games, so I told her that Big Jack wanted us to do it against Wimbledon as it was proving so successful.

I will never forget the sight of her coming off that train. She was wearing a fur coat, with a bra and suspenders underneath, and carrying a bottle of champagne. This young lady hadn't come to Sheffield to discuss the offside law!

Having sex the night before the game was frowned upon by all managers. They were worried about lads going out drinking and clubbing rather than being tucked up in bed with a girl, but even that wasn't supposed to happen!

I remember booking the same hotel for a one-night stand before scoring a couple of goals against my old club Derby and staying over in Chesterfield before the 3-3 draw.

My date with the Wimbledon blonde fully lived up to expectations. I'll spare you the details but, yes, we had a great time. Afterwards we were relaxing in the bath when there was a sudden knock at the door. Neither of us was keen to move, but someone wasn't taking no for an answer. When I got out of the bath, I was in for a rude shock. Guests were ordered outside into the car park due to an incident nearby. Turned out that the Yorkshire Ripper had been arrested! That was a memorable night in history, yet I was more worried about the police telling Big Jack they'd seen me at the hotel with a woman!

I'm not saying what I did was right or wrong but as a way of relaxing before a game that took some beating. Footballers find it hard to sleep, so were sometimes given sleeping pills to help them nod off - not good because they can become addictive.

Having a good time with a girl never put me off my football – and worked out almost perfectly on this occasion. The woman was in the stands supposedly to watch her man but with an eye on me as I turned in a great performance. By 4.10pm on the Hillsborough clock I'd already scored twice. I forgot about passing to teammates as I tried everything to get an extra goal. I never scored a professional hat trick and had to give it the best as we eventually won 3-1. Still not a bad day and a very good weekend. Wednesday went top and I was happy.

Two more goals against Blackpool in a 4-1 win made it 20 goals in just five games for us at Hillsborough and kept us at the top of the pile. But just when you think you're invincible, football nearly always has a disappointment around the corner.

Four draws in five games was very frustrating going into the second Steel City derby at Bramall Lane. We were still in the top three whilst Blades needed a win to give them an outside shot at promotion.

We never let them forget about Boxing Day but doing the double over your neighbours isn't easy. Look at results from Merseyside derbies, Manchester United and Manchester City and Spurs and Arsenal and others over the years and you'll see what I mean.

Blades planned to stop me running riot like I did at Hillsborough. Tony Kenworthy followed me everywhere and we nearly came to blows. The game was a very rare Third Division match on Match of the Day and they focused on an incident when I gave Kenworthy a friendly slap around the face and a few words. That sort of incident is easily blown up out of all proportion these days and gets you sent off. Kenworthy took the heat out of it afterwards by telling Jimmy Hill and co. that he would happily buy me a drink if he saw me in the bar. The image projected by the media and believed by the fans wasn't the case. Kenworthy and I were bitter rivals on the pitch for 90 minutes but later got on very well as friends. When I joined Sheffield United, Tony was one of the lads who did his very best to make me welcome.

The match was predictably tight with neither side playing much football. They got themselves a first half goal and chances were rare before I scored one of the best goals of my career to get us a draw. I found out later that goal could have been a lot more famous. When I attended the end of season awards to receive my Golden Boot for being the Third Division's leading goalscorer, Match of the Day presenter, Jimmy Hill, told the audience that it could have been goal of the season but just missed the deadline. Instead the honour went to Justin Fashanu for his spectacular volley for Norwich City against Liverpool and mine didn't even get a shot at the monthly award.

Two games in three days was a tough ask after a physical battle at Bramall Lane as we struggled to beat Gillingham at Hillsborough before I went past three defenders and was sent crashing in the penalty area. Ever reliable Mark Smith strode up to put the spot kick away and that was enough for two more points.

We were on a long unbeaten run and thought that a top three finish was almost certain, but defeat at Gigg Lane against Bury with just four games left nearly gave us a late attack of the jitters.

We quickly eased any nerves with a 3-0 win over Chester, including a young Ian Rush, and followed that up with a 2-1 success at Blackburn. Owls fans then outnumbered the home crowd at Exeter in our last but one match. We all expected to win and clinch promotion in style, but it didn't work out that way. We went down to a disappointing 1-0 defeat, only to get the good news that our rivals Chesterfield also failed to win. That left us two points clear with a 12-goal better goal difference. We weren't officially up, but safe enough for the directors to pop the champagne corks in the dressing room.

The next Saturday was celebration time as more than 32,000 packed into Hillsborough for the visit of Carlisle United. Unfortunately, the occasion again fell flat as we were held to a 0-0 draw. So we had to settle for the third promotion spot on 58 points, one ahead of an unlucky Chesterfield. Between you and me, they played better football than us and didn't deserve to miss out. Sheffield United finished mid-table and 12 months later went down to the Fourth Division.

Making his way in the Carlisle side was a talented 19-year-old called Peter Beardsley. Jack spoke with me in the boot room, asking what I thought of him. I told him that I'd seen enough for us to snap him up if we could, but Big Jack shrugged his shoulders and said he was too small. A few years later Beardsley was discarded after only one appearance for Manchester United before becoming a top, top striker with Newcastle, Liverpool and England.

That was an outstanding season for me. Winning the Third Division's Golden Boot was a great honour. Add my couple in the League Cup and I ended that campaign with 24. It could have been many more but for Mark Smith taking the penalties and the nature of our football. But I look back on it with pride now that my goals played a big part in Owls ending our slump and heading back in the right direction. It was also a time when the fans started to return to Hillsborough after some barren years.

Wednesday getting promotion to the Second Division, or the Championship as it is now, was only half time – and I'm sure Big Jack felt that way too. But we disagreed about how to go all the way to Division One. He favoured giving the players who got us promoted their chance. I wanted a few new signings to give us a lift.

A good start in the league, following a 2-0 opening day win over Newcastle United at Hillsborough and another Bramall Lane goal for me in a 3-1 win over two legs against the Blades in the League Cup – took the pressure off the need for change.

My season took a turn for the worse on a day that Wednesday fans still talk about at Oldham Athletic. I pulled a few tricks in my career and saw red but this time I wasn't guilty. Sometimes referees have your number and George Courtney had mine. In all, he sent me off four of the five times that I was dismissed in professional football. He totally bought a piece of play acting from Simon Stainrod, who stopped me taking a quick throw by pushing me in the chest. I brought my knee up as if to kick him between his legs and Stainrod went sprawling on the ground. But I never touched him. I pulled out to avoid contact only for Courtney to come marching over with a red card. Stainrod winked and smiled and that's what started off the riot.

Next thing we knew fans were invading the pitch, throwing debris from the terraces. A bad incident quickly got a lot worse. Big Jack appealed for calm on the pitch and nearly got hit himself. It was a sad, sad sight to see him in tears in the dressing room. He was ashamed of what was going on in Sheffield Wednesday's name. The pitch invasion made the Saturday night news and got Wednesday and me into big trouble.

First came a typical FA disciplinary hearing led by chairman, Bert Millichip, the kind of bloke that all the FA jokes were meant for. Before going into the hearing in Soho, Big Jack warned me not to say anything and to let him speak. I was confident of getting the red card overturned. As they were talking about the Stainrod incident, I tried to interrupt to give my side of the story, but Big Jack tapped me under the table to keep quiet.

I got a four-match suspension and a hefty ban for Stainrod's dive which took me over the points limit. I lost it and told Millichip that I was going to the newspapers to say how disappointed I was at the way the matter had been handled. Millichip responded by threatening a longer ban and a bigger fine. Big Jack assured Millichip that he would keep me quiet.

As we were coming out of the hearing, I had a microphone pointed towards my face by none other than David Icke, then a BBC sports presenter, having been briefly a professional goalkeeper with Coventry City. He kept asking questions, but I said nothing.

Hillsborough's terraces were locked down for four games as part of the punishment which got me a rollocking from Owls chairman Bert McGhee. But when he was in full throttle, I told him that I'd done him and the club a favour – closed terraces meant more fans paying for seats and more revenue for Owls. That brought a smile back to his face!

Nobody wants a pitch invasion but, in a way, it was a compliment to me. I was the fans' favourite, so when I got sent off for nothing, it tipped them over the edge. It got ugly, but nobody got hurt and time's a great healer – I've got lots of respect for Stainrod, the cheating bastard. Only joking!

When you're at rock bottom and been kicked in the teeth, there's never any shortage of people to rub it in. I was an easy target for being an unpredictable, volatile type – neutrals were never going to believe me against the media. At least I found out who my real friends were. Bally, then manager of Blackpool, wrote in the press that I was an honest lad and would have been horrified by what happened. He was right!

I returned from suspension just in time to experience the game without fans on the terraces. Blackburn Rovers were in town when I gave cameraman, Steve Ellis, a snap to savour. I had a feeling that I would score – I needed one as I hadn't broken my duck that season.

The goal was typical Owls. Long clearance, flick on by Andy McCulloch and I raced clear to lob over the goalkeeper. Momentum took me on towards the non-existent fans as I sunk on my knees to celebrate what turned out to be the winner. Couldn't help it. I was that kind of showman!

There was plenty to celebrate for all of us during the first half of the season as we won our first six home matches to close within a couple of points of early leaders, West Ham United, in October. That became a still handy fifth place by Christmas and, after I scored a couple to take out my revenge on Oldham and we saw off Swansea City and QPR, Owls were in the third promotion spot with only a dozen games left.

Draws against Cardiff and Derby didn't do much to dent our hopes of a second successive promotion, but getting beaten by Blackburn Rovers and Orient were big setbacks. Luckily, the return of the Match of the Day cameras for the visit of David Pleat's Luton Town saw the best of Wednesday and me. Ante Mirocevic got himself a goal and I tucked away a couple of chances in the second half as we triumphed. This left us only a point adrift of third place Swansea with a game in hand.

The wheels really came off and tension between me and Big Jack came to boiling point the following week at Wrexham. We were confident of turning them over at the Racecourse Ground but got hammered 4-0. Jack went crazy. Tea went everywhere as the bollocking started. Big Jack wasn't shy of handing out stick to individual players and I usually got the worst of it. Perhaps it was because I was a high profile player who had plenty to say. He let rip and I gave him plenty back. I reminded him of what I said all along – three more signings could have made the difference between challenging and getting ourselves promoted. Let's just say, he wasn't in the mood to agree with me!

It was all downhill from there and four defeats in our last four games meant that, after being so close to the top three nearly all the way, we finished in mid-table with 42 points from as many games. We only managed six points from our last dozen games, more like relegation than promotion form.

I got myself 11 goals that season - not bad as I was mostly playing out wide. We won 14 games at Hillsborough which kept our home fans happy, but lost the same number away where we were nearly always well supported.

That summer Big Jack asked me to do him a favour by playing for Swedish club Atvidabergs. It was then that I found out what former England manager Sven-Goran Erikkson knew – the football in Sweden is a bit boring, but the women are fantastic.

It was a bonus that I received a £5,000 signing on fee and paid £500 a week, higher than any club I played for, except Everton. I even met up with Frank 'Elvis' Worthington for three or four days as he was playing for Norrkoping. We had a great time; Frank was exactly like he was on the field – larger than life, totally genuine and down-to-earth, someone who really enjoyed himself once the game was over. And, yes, he loved Elvis Presley.

I enjoyed my time in Sweden and, looking back, I think that was one of Big Jack's money saving ideas. Whilst I was abroad, Wednesday weren't paying my wages, but it nearly cost the club my registration. Jack phoned to say 'see you back here next week' but the Swedish manager knew nothing about it and wanted me there until the end of their season. I don't know what happened but within a couple of days the argument was sorted and I was on my way back to Wednesday, ready for pre-season where Big Jack presented me with a new contract on the same terms.

The signing of Gary Bannister, a forward who showed promise at Coventry, gave me a lift. Now we had two players who could combine down the flanks and give McCulloch support up front. Like me, Gary had a trick and took defenders out of the game. We also had more natural ability in the middle of the park with Gary Megson joining Ante Mirocevic, Brian Hornsby and Denis Lehman. We had the potential to play more football – at least in my opinion.

Defensively we had plenty of strength, although big Jim Holton, the former Manchester United centre back, suffered through injury. Peter Shirtliff, Mick Pickering, Mark Smith and Mel Sterland were in the squad and there was plenty of young talent coming through in John Pearson, Trevor Matthews and Gavin Oliver.

When I asked Big Jack why his fantastic Leeds United never won as many trophies as they should, he said that their weakness was in goal where Gary Sprake made important mistakes. It was the same at Wednesday. I'm not being over critical of Bob Bolder because he was a good bloke and a fair goalkeeper, but there was a mistake in him and I think that we could have strengthened that position.

Success and failure in football is decided by 'small margins' and that applied to my final season at Hillsborough. We missed out by one point after again cocking up late in the season. That single point took my career along a different course. I'd have put my differences with the manager to one side for the chance to play for Sheffield Wednesday in the First Division. But another late collapse only added to my frustration.

I was again disappointed that we weren't adventurous enough and didn't play to my strengths. My running battle with the boss was wanting the ball played to my feet or just in front, so I could run onto it and take on a defender. Instead, we continued to hump the ball forward and chase after it. We spent so much time and energy trying to win the ball back or frustrate the opposition after we'd kicked away possession.

I was a good runner. I could do cross country and was one of the best at the club. But I was best, razor sharp, over 10 metre sprints. That was all that I needed to get at the opposition defence and put them on the back foot. Instead, I was often running several times that distance back and forward, trying to get a foot in.

It was a shame for the fans who were brilliant during my three years at Hillsborough. The support we took to away games, in both the Third and Second Division, was breathtaking. It made the hairs stand up on the back of my neck running out at fairly modest grounds and seeing the terraces packed with Wednesday fans. There was joy and laughter and the noise was deafening. Whatever was happening in my private life was forgotten when I pulled on the famous blue and white striped shirt.

We made the perfect start with four successive league wins without conceding a goal. The bookies quickly took notice, making us 3-1 favourites for the title. I was in good form, scoring the winner at Blackburn on opening day and creating all three as we gave Luton another hammering at Kenilworth Road. That was when Big Jack described me as 'the most exciting player in the Football League'.

Despite suffering our first defeat at Barnsley, we were still top of the table come the end of September before things began to dip. We got heavily beaten again at Wrexham and blitzed by a Simon Stainrod hat trick for QPR. We then slipped to sixth when losing 2-1 by Chelsea at Stamford Bridge.

A cold blast meant that we didn't play again until January 16 and needed a lift. My relationship with the manager took a big dive whilst training in the gym before the trip to Norwich City. It must have been cold because that was the only time we did that at Hillsborough. My Wednesday mate, Mel Sterland, tells the story of what happened next – well, he got it about three quarters right!

Jack was at the other end of the gym, having come through the bottom door entrance. He shouted out loud to me: "You're playing on the wing tomorrow at Norwich."

I barked back that I wasn't - the worst thing you can say to a manager. The shouting match continued before Jack took big, long strides towards me, his face red with anger. Remember Jack's six foot three and I'm five feet ten and a half. As he was getting closer, Jack started to take off his sheepskin coat and I was thinking that we were going to get into a fight here. I'd seen lots of them in training but never fallen out with any of my teammates.

Jack's coat was off by the time he was about two feet away with spit coming out of his mouth. Jack said again that I was playing out wide and I said I wasn't. It was Jack who threw the first punch. I ducked to miss the punch then, with Jack now even closer, grabbed him by his waist and lifted him over my shoulder. We both fell onto the gym floor throwing punches at each other. The other lads jumped in to break it up although I heard Mel shouting to leave us to fight! I was left out at Carrow Road as we won 3-2.

Shortly after that we went on a run of six wins in seven matches putting us in a great position to clinch promotion after all. We were six points clear in the third promotion spot with Norwich, who eventually pipped us, nine points adrift with a game in hand.

The press, however, had other things on their minds with many column inches being written about the state of my relationship with Big Jack. The general view was that come May and I was out of contract that I'd be on my way. I put that on hold expecting us to finish off the job. Unfortunately, what followed was one of the biggest disappointments of my life.

It all started with a crushing 4-0 defeat at Watford whilst Norwich began a run of four successive wins. Draws against Chelsea and Rotherham followed, but we were still confident of getting over the line as the Canaries had to come to Hillsborough in the last game.

Norwich were a point in front with two matches left. We were at Bolton and they were at Orient. Things weren't going too badly at half time as I scored one of my rare goals that season to leave us at 1-1. But disaster happened in the second half as we went down 3-1 and Norwich won.

So, after being nine points back, Norwich were promoted with a game to spare and we had blown it. We beat them 2-1 on the last day but that merely rubbed in our disappointment.

That failure was the last straw for me at Wednesday, along with the problems that I had negotiating a new deal with Jack. With neither club agreeing on a transfer fee, it went to a messy tribunal that didn't do either of us any good.

Big Jack offered to give me what I wanted and even revealed that First Division Everton had offered £500,00 for me but it was all too late.

He might not have been so conciliatory had he known I'd just taken a new woman on holiday to Newquay before returning to Sheffield. The idea was then to attend the tribunal – which fixed the transfer fee at £100,000 and to sign for Sheffield United the next day.

In the tribunal were Big Jack, Bert McGhee, Reg Brealey and Ian Porterfield, Blades manager. Wednesday were asking £500,000 because Big Jack had brought in a fax from Everton offering the same money. But the final figure was much lower because it took into account that Owls bought me for £100,000, my wages had been £300 a week and the offer that Owls made didn't match their valuation of me.

There was one more late intervention when I took a phone call from Newcastle United manager, Arthur Cox. He was tempted by the transfer fee and asked whether I had signed yet. Then he offered me a whopping £150,000 signing on fee and £800 a week. He told me that he wanted a forward line of me and Chris Waddle on the flanks with Kevin Keegan and Peter Beardsley down the middle.

Sounded great, but I wasn't interested. Money was never a major issue in my thinking and, say what you like about me, once I've shaken hands on a deal, I stick with it.

So, a lifelong Wednesdayite was on his way to Bramall Lane! Even now I can hardly believe it. I put my differences with the manager and my love for life in Sheffield above my football career and dropped a clanger by again dropping into the Third Division.

Most Wednesday fans have forgiven me but I'm not sure I have ever forgiven myself. None of us can turn the clock back but I wish I had stayed at Hillsborough and played in the First Division for them.

CHAPTER FOUR
WINNING HOWARD'S WAY

Extract from an article by former Everton manager HOWARD KENDALL

SOMETIMES an individual can spark a team into life and get the maximum from the players around him.

One of the best examples I ever brought in was Terry Curran. The team was struggling and I initially brought the lad in on loan from Sheffield United.

He was looking forward to the challenge and to gaining a permanent deal. He made an immediate impact and gave the place a lift.

Terry was direct, technically good and most importantly he wanted the ball. That kind of attitude rubs off on the other players.

Results picked up and notably so did the performances of his teammates.

*****

By John BAILEY, Everton defender 1979-1986

HOWARD Kendall brought Terry in when we were struggling at Everton and he gave the whole place a lift. He had a great loan spell with us and then signed permanently from Sheffield United.

Terry was part of our side that had so much success, yet it so nearly never happened. You could see the words 'Kendall out' everywhere in 1984 and the story goes that the manager would have been sacked had we lost a League Cup tie at Oxford United. Terry and I were out injured that night when Adrian Heath scrambled a late equaliser and it all turned round from there.

Terry was a terrific footballer who created a lot of goals for Andy Gray, but he was also important off the pitch. He came in with a lot of confidence when we needed it most and did well for us both at home and in Europe when we eventually won the European Cup Winners' Cup.

He was one of the lads and I'll always remember him being the first to celebrate with me in the tunnel after we beat Southampton to reach the FA Cup final.

He socialised with the rest of us and was great fun to be with. He had a few football clubs in his career, almost as many as the night clubs we went to in Southport. He also loved going into the boutiques and shops, dressing up in leather and chatting up pretty women.

I'm going to be honest – he had a temper on him. When we heard the door smash shut after he had been in the manager's office, I knew he was in a mood. It was usually because he'd been left out of the side, but he soon came round again.

We were a top side on the pitch and enjoyed life to the full off it and Terry was a part of both.

*****

MY life would also have been easier had I gone straight from Wednesday to Everton.

It was never going to work out for me at Sheffield United although I'm no Blades hater. When producing my version of *Singing the Blues* I refused to sing the line 'and United lose'. I didn't want to add more fuel to the fire as some supporters go over the top.

The key to me going to Bramall Lane was that I shook hands on the deal with chairman Reg Brealey, including £50,000 in two payments as a signing on fee. I knew that other clubs were interested, but I took the bait.

The other reason that I went to Sheffield United was because I loved the city. I enjoyed going out in Sheffield and was more than happy to stay there. All in all, I loved the life in Sheffield.

I had history with Sheffield United after destroying them at Forest and tormenting them with Wednesday. Blades fans never forgot my man of the match performance in the 4-0 Boxing Day massacre or my running battle with Tony Kenworthy and the spectacular equalising goal in the return at Bramall Lane.

I could have been a big success for Sheffield United despite the hostility which the move generated among both sets of supporters. The United players did their best to make me welcome. Tony Kenworthy and John McPhail, who tried to maim me when I wore blue and white, were two of the friendliest and striker Alan Young also became a mate.

I never hit it off with Keith Edwards, who was something of a Blades legend. A selfish striker in the Gary Lineker mould, he'd helped himself to 35 goals the previous season and perhaps didn't fancy sharing the limelight with a player who he regarded as a Wednesdayite.

Brealey was good to me and wanted to get something back on his investment, but the main obstacle to me at Bramall Lane was manager Ian Porterfield, who made it clear that he never wanted me at the club despite the fact we had played together at Wednesday. He put his own signings, Colin Morris and Tony Towner, in front of me, whom he regarded as Reg Brealey's men. He certainly didn't like the fact that Reg not only talked to me but also invited me to his house in Spalding. I liked Reg very much as a person and saw him as a good contact and a way into management later in my career.

Playing Third Division football again wasn't good for my career, but I knew I could do anything that I set my mind to. It didn't help though that I was going through marital problems during my spell with Sheffield United. Footballers say off-field issues don't affect their game and it's true you forget it all when the whistle blows. But when you are going through a difficult time, it can't help the way you do your job.

I played 33 times for Sheffield United and thought that I did reasonably well in a poor team. One thing I can assure United fans, I put in the same effort that I always did once I crossed that white line. Fans accused me of not caring because my heart was with Owls, but that wasn't true. I wanted to win every football match that I played in and that was no different when I played for The Blades.

Porterfield did do me a favour four months into my contract when he said First Division Everton were interested in taking me on loan. "Get me out of here as quickly as you can," I said. The chance to play again in the topflight even for a month was a no-brainer. To sweeten the blow for Blades, Trevor Ross moved on loan from Everton to United.

It was almost inevitable that I'd end up on Merseyside at some stage as Everton had first courted me during my Doncaster Rovers' days. When I walked into Goodison Park, I couldn't believe my eyes. The facilities were top class, far better than at any other club that I'd played for – a training pitch, gym, sauna the lot. I knew from the moment that I set foot in the place this was a fantastic football club.

Everything was in their favour with Toffees legend, Howard Kendall, managing a team full of talent and potential. But, for whatever reason, it was all going wrong. Talking with Kendall at his home, there were hangmen daubed in paint on his garage wall with the words 'death to Kendall'. It's difficult to believe and frightening at times how far fans go when things aren't going well.

After a few good early results, a run of eight games without a win had seen them slump to 15th and get dumped out of the League Cup. To make things worse, they lost 5-0 to Liverpool who, as usual, were flying.

Attendances at Goodison Park had dropped alarmingly before I joined. They only just topped 13,000 for a League Cup tie against Arsenal. Kendall told me that the team needed a lift, a new face in the dressing room to get them out of the rut. I knew I was joining them at the right time. The only way for this set of lads was up. And I had the confidence to believe that I could help.

Playing at a lower level hadn't dented my self belief in any way. As people told me, I was always better suited playing with top class players. I lost count of those who told me that I was far too good for the Third Division. I was 28 years old and determined to prove that I could still cut it at the highest level. The Everton loan gave me nothing to lose and everything to gain. My mind was fully focused on doing everything that I could to ensure a First Division future for Terry Curran.

Morale was low and the confidence wasn't there but none of that bothered me. I always wanted the ball whether the team was winning or losing. I hadn't been at Goodison Park long as things started to go downhill, so wasn't affected by the low crowds and the poor results. I know that I helped bring confidence and smiles back to those players during my loan.

My Toffees' debut against Ron Saunders' defensive-minded Birmingham City wasn't the best game of all time. It wasn't even the best 0-0 draw, but I did well enough to feel pleased with myself and please Kendall and the fans. Duncan McKenzie, a player with some similarities to me and an Everton hero, said that he enjoyed seeing me give big Pat Van Den Hauwe a chasing. The attendance for that game was 13,707.

That blank meant that a team including Kevin Sheedy, David Johnson, Adrian Heath, Andy King and Steve McMahon hadn't scored in four games.

Facing Bobby Robson's very good Ipswich Town side at Portman Road, with Paul Cooper, George Burley, Terry Butcher, Franz Thijssen, Paul Mariner, Alan Brazil and all the rest, may have been daunting for some Everton lads, but was an exciting challenge for me. That night proved a turning point for Everton as I set up goals for both Kevin Richardson and Sheedy in a 2-0 win. Skipper Kevin Ratcliffe encouraged the lads in the dressing room at half time to give me the ball as I was ripping them apart.

That burst the bubble of not finding the net and not winning, but did little to inspire the Goodison Park faithful. Only 14,982 turned out on the next Saturday afternoon for the visit of Luton Town. But those that did went home with the clear message that both Everton and Terry Curran were back in business.

That was the day I showed Everton fans and Kendall what I could do as we overwhelmed David Pleat's men 5-0. I scored my first Everton goal and made two more to become an instant hit with the supporters. The goal that I scored was one of my best at the top level. It was early in the second half when I picked up the ball just inside our half, ran at speed at the Luton defence and placed my shot beyond the diving goalkeeper from just outside the penalty area. The feeling was fantastic. I was back in the big time.

Everton fans sung 'sign him up, sign him up' and 'let's have a whip round' and the manager and chairman, Phil Carter, were both full of praise for me afterwards. It could have been even better had the referee not been fooled by a Luton defender in the first half. I was past him with a clear run in on goal when I was sent sprawling. Commentator Martin Tyler agreed with the referee that I had dived but hadn't seen the full back flick out his left foot which caught me and sent me off balance.

I was always an honest player who never dived. That wasn't my style. As a forward who ran at defenders at pace, it takes only the slightest touch. But I always tried to stay on my feet and score rather than fool the referee.

That sent us into the hectic Christmas period of four league matches in eight days in great spirits. I was having a good time of my own off the field, living in a hotel after persuading my girlfriend that she was better off staying in Sheffield.

I went back to her for Christmas Day before we trained on Boxing Day and went to Stoke City on December 27. There we had a reality check as we were beaten 1-0 by a goal from England winger, Mark Chamberlain. It was a difficult afternoon trying to get any change out of Stoke's formidable defensive duo of George Berry and Dave Watson. They weren't a bad side with the likes of Sammy Mcilroy and Mickey Thomas also among their ranks.

We needed another lift when we entertained Nottingham Forest the following day. Playing against Cloughie's lot was always a big occasion for me and this was the first time that I was on the winning side against my old boss. They were nothing like the side that won the First Division and two European Cups but were still second in the league before kick off.

To be honest we gave them a good pasting in front of a much improved crowd of more than 25,000. We were three goals up and cruising with two goals for Graeme Sharp and one for Steve McMahon by the time Steve Hodge got one back for Forest. It was a particularly good day for me as I was up against Bryn Gunn, the young Forest player who I made my debut with at the City Ground. There was no doubt that I had the better of him and Cloughie was impressed enough to have a message for me when I left the pitch.

"Young man," he said. "Why don't you come and play for me again – you were special today?" That was one of the occasions when he asked me outright to return to Forest. I was only on loan at Everton but was already looking to have a future there. Forest were higher in the league but I thought that Everton was the one with a big future – and that's how it turned out.

New Year's Day saw me give a chasing to a very good full back, West Brom's Derek Statham, in an entertaining game at The Hawthorns. Mark Higgins and Sharpy scored for us but we had to be content with a point from a 2-2 draw. I had a lot of respect for Statham. I rated him on a par with Kenny Sansom as the best full back I played against. As it happened, Sansom made 86 appearances for the full England side and Statham just three. Whilst writing this book, Statham wrote on social media that I was one of his most difficult opponents – and I knew it!

Two days later I played my seventh game in just 27 days and it was disappointing to end my brief spell on Merseyside in losing fashion as, despite another goal from Sharpy, we went down 2-1 to Tottenham Hotspur at White Hart Lane.

We'd moved up a few places in the league, attracted a few thousand fans back to Goodison Park and beaten a couple of good sides. I helped Everton to raise their spirits and confidence and it was very tough having to go back to Bramall lane at the end of my month on loan.

At least I had the excitement of the FA Cup to inspire me and, after a 0-0 draw at home to Stoke City, I put in by far my best Blades performance in the Potteries in the replay. I paralysed a very good defence that night as I set up a couple of goals for Edwards before we eventually went out 3-2.

There was plenty of interest from the top clubs after my spell at Everton and ideally, I wanted to join them permanently. They agreed a £100,000 fee with Sheffield United but that's as far as it went.

Kendall invited me to Birch Services off the M62 for talks. He wanted me back to boost his side who were still very up and down, but I was disappointed with his terms. He offered £500 a week, plus a £10,000 signing on fee. I was there with a friend of mine, Gerry Webster, a big Owls fan who ran my fan club. I told Kendall that I wanted the £25,000 in my contract and £1,000 a week.

Kendall appealed to me by saying: "Who do you want to play for? Everton in the First Division or Sheffield United in the Third?"

I said that it didn't make any difference whether it was Everton, Sheffield United or Halifax if I was playing football, but I wasn't going to accept £10,000 from Everton when I had £25,000 in my contract with Blades. I wanted to be paid what I was worth and told Kendall that I had saved him from the sack.

Things got more complicated with Arsenal and Manchester United joining the chase. United were particularly attractive to me as I'd always liked them due to George Best and their European Cup winning days. Their approach didn't come from manager, Ron Atkinson, but a tabloid reporter called Norman Winn who phoned to say that United were interested. Next came Don Howe at Arsenal and suddenly, Brealey thought that he was onto a good thing and increased my asking price from £100,000 to £500,000.

The way it was handled by Porterfield and Brealey disappointed me. Manchester United were keen to sign a wide man and set a deadline to complete the deal. Blades played for time and United turned instead to Arthur Graham. It was a similar story with Arsenal as they eventually settled for Brian Marwood from Hull City. Meanwhile Everton were put off by the higher fee.

The auction that never happened meant that I was left to see out the rest of the season with The Blades. As Porterfield didn't want me and the team wasn't firing that was difficult. Having had a sniff of First Division football again, it was even harder to refocus.

Thankfully, all was in place in the summer to move me on. Everton, who were still not reaching their real potential, offered a permanent deal meaning that I would clear £1,000 a week – the best money of my career. I was on my way back to Goodison Park.

The lads had won only one of their first four games of the 1983/84 season, but I was confident that Everton could turn it around. I was excited about making my second debut against West Brom, but the game ended in big disappointment. My injury at Forest played a huge part in my career and the thigh injury that I suffered at Everton was another crushing setback. I was out of action for five months and never got to play as regularly as I wanted for one of the best teams of that generation.

To be honest, I don't think I did myself any favours the summer before I joined Everton when I ran a marathon for charity in Sheffield. As I've said, I was always more of a sprinter than a long distance runner, although I held my own at cross country. But I had never run 26 miles-plus before. I was going well up to 18 miles which is where many 'hit the wall'. I jogged and walked the last eight, eventually making it over the line after more than six hours. It was all about finishing and I wasn't bothered about being one of the last to complete the course. What that did to my body though is another matter. My legs were very stiff for a good four days and that could well have contributed to my thigh injury.

Even when I was out of the side, I did Kendall a favour when he was about to sell Peter Reid. Reidy was the worst trainer that I came across in my life and that may have been why the boss was prepared to let him go. But here was a player with natural ability to read the game and perform when it really mattered. I told Kendall that Reidy was by far his best midfield player.

Reidy came out of the manager's office with a slight tear in his eye, telling me: "Howard says he has had an offer from Burnley – and I can go if I want to." I knew Reidy liked it at Everton and told him from my own experience of too many moves that he didn't have to go.

I was due to see Kendall to update my injury situation but told him in no uncertain terms: "You'll regret it if you sell him to Burnley. He's the player who makes us tick – he reads the game and puts us on the front foot." I'm not sure that Everton would have achieved half the success that followed if we had sold Peter Reid.

It's funny how things happen in football and that night at Oxford United in the quarter final of the League Cup was a great example of why clubs sometimes need to show more patience with managers.

I knew what a terrific manager Howard Kendall was, but he was so close to getting the sack. There was nothing I could do about it as I was still out injured when we faced Jim Smith's highly competitive Third Division side who had already knocked out Newcastle, Leeds and Manchester United.

Neville Southall was the busier of the two goalkeepers before Bobby McDonald shot Oxford ahead in the 67th minute. Everton looked to be on their way out before my mate Adrian Heath latched onto a bad back pass eight minutes from time to earn us a replay.

I tried desperately to get myself fit when we reached the final against Liverpool. I got as far as a reserve match at Barnsley, but was forced to sit on the sidelines as the lads went down 1-0 after a replay.

There was still something for me and the team to play for, however, as we were going strong in the FA Cup. I finally got myself back into the side just before the semi final against my old club Saints at Highbury, creating a goal for Derek Mountfield in a 3-0 win at Luton, then facing up to Kenny Sansom for another valuable 90 minutes in a draw against Arsenal.

I was excited about getting the chance to put one over on my old boss, McMenemy, when I got the nod to start. It was a very tense afternoon with both master goalkeepers, Neville Southall and Peter Shilton, keeping their sides in it at different stages. I nearly set up Adrian Heath only for his effort to be cleared off the line by Mick Mills and sent in another cross that Andy Gray couldn't quite get on the end of.

My legs were extra weary going into extra time after so little football, but Kendall kept faith. Finally, I started the move that led to Peter Reid winning and taking the free kick from which Heath scrambled in the winning goal three minutes from the whistle. I celebrated in style by going clubbing in Southport with John Bailey, Andy Gray and Heath, who tried in vain to interest all the pretty girls in his winning goal.

My thoughts were on a second chance to play at Wembley and there was a good month to go to get some valuable game time into my legs. Games came thick and fast until disaster struck three weeks before the cup final when I pulled a hamstring at Norwich. Maybe I could have been used more sparingly but I've got no complaints. There wasn't the sports science that is available now and I was desperate to play after being out for most of the season.

I think I would have been in Kendall's plans for the match against Elton John's Watford.

So for the second time an Everton FA Cup final win pulled at my heart strings. This was the first time that Everton had won the cup since that 1966 success against Wednesday and, although I was delighted for the lads, I would have loved to have been there. Inchy (Adrian Heath) visited me in Southport to show me his medal after we beat the Hornets 2-0.

I rated Kendall almost as highly as Brian Clough. People got the wrong impression of his drinking. I saw much more evidence of Kendall hitting the booze than Cloughie, yet it never affected his job. He was always sharp on match days when we needed him.

The socialising at Everton was legendary with my roommate, John Bailey, being one of the main drinkers. I picked him up to go to training on Monday morning knowing that he would have had a few. The lads knew that there was less chance of getting into trouble because Kendall was in the same boat.

Kendall was one of the few managers who looked good on the training ground and wasn't a ranter or raver. If we were struggling at half time, the boss made a few useful tactical points rather than throwing stuff around. Like Cloughie, he didn't fill our heads with endless material about the opposition but encouraged us to go out and play our passing, high tempo game.

The summer gave me time to prepare for the 1984-85 season which turned out to be one of the most momentous in the club's history.

It was even harder to get into the starting line up after Kendall pulled a masterstroke in signing Trevor Steven from Burnley. Trevor was 20 years old when Kendall brought him in but quickly repaid his faith. A much different kind of wide man to me, he went on to play more than 200 matches for Everton and win 36 England caps.

I got a fair crack of the action early in our First Division title winning season which, ironically, started with a 4-1 defeat at home to Spurs and a 2-1 loss at West Brom.

It was also exciting to play European football for the first time when I appeared in both legs of the first round tie against University College, Dublin. The tie was watched by barely 25,000 fans over the two legs and we so nearly went out. After drawing the away tie 0-0, Graeme Sharp put us ahead early in the return, but we were left on a knife edge as an equaliser would have put the underdogs through on away goals.

As Everton's season soared, mine nosedived after giving the linesman a volley of abuse in a 5-4 defeat against Watford at Vicarage Road. I only came on in the 90th minute and still managed to get myself sent off.

I got 10 minutes as a substitute when we thrashed Cloughie's Forest 5-0 at Goodison Park. The hectic Christmas schedule of four games in nine days saw me get a couple of starts as we began a 28-game unbeaten run in all competitions. I helped Sharpy net the winner at Ipswich then hit the woodwork as we saw off high flying Luton Town 2-1 at Goodison Park. A less eventful appearance from the bench in the return game against Watford was my only first team action for a while as the lads reeled off nine successive wins.

But I was still in Kendall's thoughts, starting both legs against Dutch side, Fortuna Sittard in Europe, as we cruised to a 5-0 aggregate victory. Sadly though, the dream semi-final against German giants, Bayern Munich, shut the door on my Everton career without me kicking a ball.

It came about because I was desperate to play. I thought that I was in with a shout to start the very difficult first leg in Munich as both Andy Gray and Kevin Sheedy were struggling with injuries. But when the bibs were handed out at the end of the training session – and I didn't get one – I went to see Kendall to ask him straight up.

He told me that he was still thinking about his team, but that wasn't good enough for me. I decided there and then, that if I was going to be substitute at best, I wasn't going to the airport. And I stuck to my guns. Some of the other lads tried to talk me out of it, especially Reidy as his kit was in my car! That meant I'd kicked my last ball for Everton who went on to beat Munich and lift the cup by beating Rapid Vienna 3-1 in the final in Rotterdam.

My consolation was a medal for being part of a brilliant title winning side. The lads also reached another FA Cup final which meant yet another afternoon on the sofa instead of playing, as our hopes of a double were ended by Norman Whiteside's brilliant goal for Manchester United.

CHAPTER FIVE
MY LAST LEGS AND A LIFE LESSON

MY FOOTBALL life may have turned out very differently had I been able to take up the offer of being player manager at Halifax Town. I was struggling with my knees and moving towards full time management and coaching made perfect sense. I know that, given the right opportunity, I could have been very successful.

The move to The Shay never came about because Howard Kendall demanded a fee and that was the deal breaker. So instead, I continued my playing career with another West Yorkshire club, Second Division Huddersfield Town.

Playing for Mick Buxton, another old school long ball merchant, wasn't ideal, but I thoroughly enjoyed the 1985/86 season at Leeds Road. Buxton was straight with me from the start. His team were establishing themselves after promotion from the Third Division and the manager wanted me for one season to help them avoid being relegated.

I played through the pain in more than 30 league games and netted seven league goals, plus another in the League Cup. As I walked in the door, Sam Allardyce was on his way out. But there were a few top players in the Huddersfield squad, including former Liverpool and Wales defender, Joey Jones and centre half Paul Jones, who I played against when he was at Bolton Wanderers.

Highlights included scoring against Leeds United in the Yorkshire derby when I celebrated by bowing to all sides of the ground. I was also pleased to score a couple of first half goals against Lawrie McMenemy's Sunderland, not thinking that the following season I'd be playing for him again. Being forced to come off at half time stopped me chasing that elusive hat trick.

Revisiting Bramall Lane gave me one last chance to haunt The Blades and I had a particularly good game. The icing on the cake was a jinking run in the second half to set up the equaliser for David Cox in a 1-1 draw. Cortisone injections kept me going through the bad winter and I had another high when I grabbed the winner against Hull City,

My relationship with Buxton was up and down. Like a lot of managers back then, he bored me going over how good the opposition was. One day he went on and on about Carlisle United's 'superstars'. The left back was brilliant, midfielder a maestro and there was a goal machine up front. I could see, after about 45 minutes of this nonsense, that some of the lads were equally disinterested – but, as usual, I was the one to speak my mind.

When asked whether we had any questions, I said: "Yes, boss, remind me who we are playing against? Brazil?" He didn't take my joke very well, but it was probably what the rest of the team were thinking.

Another setback with Buxton happened after striker Duncan Shearer came in from Chelsea and scored a hat trick against Barnsley. We were playing Blackburn and Duncan was getting angry about the manager barking stupid instructions from the touchline. He asked me to help, so I told Buxton to 'f------shut up!"

We easily achieved our aim without flirting with relegation, but I wish that I could have ended my time at Leeds Road better. It was all set up for me because I had a good record against Wimbledon – both on and off the pitch!

A lot of the football world fell in love with Wimbledon because they were the underdogs. They went on a fantastic run from the Southern League to the First Division and a lot of neutrals loved it when they shocked mighty Liverpool to win the FA Cup at Wembley in 1985.

How the hell Vinnie Jones wasn't sent off for his disgraceful tackle on Steve McMahon in the early stages of that FA Cup final - only the referee will ever know. Had he brought out the red card, Wimbledon would probably have been well beaten. But those were days when sendings off in a cup final were very rare. It was amazing that more legs weren't broken or careers ended by Vinnie and his mates. It was a shame in some ways because Wimbledon did have individuals with genuine ability, such as Dennis Wise and Terry Phelan. Most of the rest were cloggers.

People who liked Vinnie Jones, John Fashanu, Wise and co. never played against them. Not sure many players from my generation can honestly say that they enjoyed going to Plough Lane. Football is for men not boys, but the lengths they went to intimidate and cheat were ridiculous. The ghetto blaster was on full volume to make life as difficult as possible for the opposition in their own dressing room. Then, in the tunnel and on the pitch for the warm up, they were full of murderous threats of what they were going to do to us. The showers were about as warm as the general welcome.

Most teams had a hard man or two in their team and I always expected to get a few kicks from a full back but dangerous tackles from Wimbledon players flew in from every area of the pitch – including up front. There was a very thin line between being 'street-wise' and thugs.

I was never frightened by them because I wasn't that kind of player. The idea was to target the opposition's most talented players and hope, after they had been kicked once or twice, that they wouldn't come back for more. I was the opposite.

They did, however, do me good and proper with another tactic – winding players up so they'd lose their temper and get sent off. And that's what happened to me on the last day at Leeds Road.

Wise pulled me back as I went on a run and I could see Fashanu, a top karate man, rushing towards me. Trying to push Wise, I accidentally caught Fashanu in the face. The toughest of hard guys, he went down like a sack of potatoes and, needless to say, George Courtney bought it and sent me off. Wimbledon wouldn't have lasted five minutes in today's football when VAR gives officials a second look at questionable tackles.

At the end of the season an offer of £600 a week tempted me and former Manchester City star, Gary Owen, to sign for the Greek side Panionios. It seemed a dream move, the perfect way to see out my playing days as my girlfriend and I settled into a beautiful hotel, complete with swimming pool and fantastic sea views and enjoyed red hot temperatures.

That was the best part of the deal as it soon became clear that we were both being taken for a ride. I had always taken the financial side of the game for granted, knowing that my wages would be paid. I was used to playing for clubs where I could concentrate fully on the football. That didn't happen in Greece. After we hadn't been paid for two or three weeks and a players' strike delayed the start of the league season, we had a chat. Gary was also worried about whether we would be paid. I decided to give it another week before booking the next flight back home.

On my last night at the hotel, I got my revenge on the club. When we came down for dinner, we noticed there were a lot of English tourists in the restaurant. Many recognised me as a footballer, so we had a chat. I told them that I'd enjoyed meeting them so much I was going to buy them all dinner. I signed to pay for all six tables and charged it to the club. I was even given a standing ovation from my new friends for being so generous. Gary rang a couple of days later to say that he had been paid, so I probably did him a favour.

With my career all but finished, I took a phone call from Hull City boss, Brian Horton, asking to help them out for a few games. Then the one-year deal at Sunderland, one of the biggest clubs that I played for in my career, came completely out of the blue.

I wasn't really expecting to get another professional contract when my Dad said that they had been on the phone. My legs were bad and I wasn't bothered about playing for them. A short time later I was in the bath when Dad took another call from Lew Chatterley. I said 'tell him I'm not interested', not wanting to play for McMenemy again. But Dad insisted that I wouldn't be playing for the manager but for Sunderland Football Club, so I decided to give it a try.

I've got to give McMenemy this: despite our rocky relationship at Southampton and a few comments in newspaper articles in the years that followed, he let bygones be bygones. At Southampton, he thrived by surrounding himself with experienced players who ran the team for him and I was one of the younger lads. Now the roles were reversed and I was 30 years old and near the end of my career.

McMenemy was looking to restore Sunderland's fortunes after they dropped out of the topflight and had several experienced players in his squad, including ex-Ipswich Town duo, George Burley and Eric Gates, Frankie Gray, who won a European Cup medal with Cloughie, former Liverpool defender, Alan Kennedy and Dave Swindlehurst up front. Unfortunately most were past their best.

It was tough going for us in the Second Division, although I did manage to score my last professional goal during my nine league appearances. I may have lasted longer but for a personal issue that finally destroyed my relationship with McMenemy.

It was a Thursday night when I took a fateful phone call from my sister-in-law Patsy with very bad news. Dad had been diagnosed with cancer and was very ill. Nobody knew how long he had left, but it was serious. I told her that I would come home after going into work the following day.

McMenemy's mind was on an important away game at St Andrews the following day as Sunderland's survival bid was in the balance. When I told him Dad had cancer and I was going home, he wasn't happy. He wanted me to play, but I said Dad was more important to me than any football match and walked out anyway.

Sunderland lost 2-0 and there wasn't much I could do for Dad either. But I would never have forgiven myself if I hadn't gone home. I had no idea how long I'd be away from Sunderland – just as long as it took.

Those were seriously unhappy days for a great football club and, after another disappointing afternoon, Gatesy rang to say that disgruntled fans had been threatening to vandalise his gold Mercedes. A few days later Chatterley said that Sunderland wanted me available as soon as possible and ordered me to play in a reserve game against Manchester City.

I didn't play many second team games in my career and this was the last thing I wanted to do. But I had no choice, so decided to travel up with my brother David and our friend Jack Hicks. My heart wasn't really in it and that played a part in what happened. Sunderland attracted a good three or four thousand to second team games and the fans were giving abuse to players that they thought were letting them down. They took it out on Paul Atkinson, one of the younger lads who had dropped down from the first team. The booing got to him so badly that when we won a free kick his confidence was shot and he asked me over to take it. I lost it completely and stuck two fingers up in the direction of the crowd. Here they were - having a go at an honest young pro doing his best when my father was fighting for something far more important – his life.

When we left the pitch, there were two police officers in the tunnel who took me to the police station for questioning. They were going to charge me for using foul and abusive language but let me go after about 20 minutes, much to the relief of David and Jack. McMenemy wasn't so forgiving. He didn't speak with me but left me to find out that I'd been kicked out of the club by reading an article in The Sun headlined Sunderland sack Curran. That was a terrible way for it all to end at a famous football club.

I couldn't talk about all the heartache behind the final rift – because that was personal to me and my family – and McMenemy never explained to the fans the circumstances that led to my dismissal.

Bobby Roberts persuaded me to join Grimsby Town even though I knew that I shouldn't have played on. My right knee was giving me a lot of pain and I'd already had more than the recommended number of cortisone injections. They numbed the pain for about five months but didn't do anything for my knee. I played a dozen or so games for Grimsby where I got a final warning from a specialist that I'd end up a cripple if I continued to play competitive sport.

Even then I answered a call from Kevin Randall, who was short of players at Chesterfield, and made my last ever professional appearance for the Spireites, ironically against Grimsby, in March 1988.

I haven't included Grantham Town in my list of clubs, but I did turn out for them a few times. I tried to do Martin O'Neill a favour in one of his first jobs in management but, to his disappointment, soon had to give up. My last games were for Goole Town during my time as manager at the Northern Premier League club.

It's very hard to quit the game that you love and nobody ends their career saying they played too many games. But I knew what my body was telling me from my time at Everton and it was only going to get worse. Fans of my last few clubs never saw me at my best and didn't see me very often. John Haselden called it right – I was as knackered at 30 years old as he was.

CHAPTER SIX
I DID IT MY WAY

By ALAN HUDSON, Chelsea, Arsenal and Stoke legend and fellow 'maverick'

I DIDN'T see too much of Terry during his playing days, but I know he was a maverick .

I'm looking here as I'm writing this at a photograph of the greatest maverick of all, Frank Worthington, who recently passed away and there were too few of them.

In my view, a team without a maverick isn't a team.

It's mavericks who put bums on seats and give fans something to talk about. I'll give you an example of what we are missing from a chat I had with some Stoke City fans before a game seven or eight years ago. I asked this young lad who he was going to watch. When he replied 'Stoke City', I asked 'which of their players are you going to watch?' and he said 'none, in particular.' That told me none of that Stoke team stood out.

England have always been reluctant to play 'mavericks'. A TV programme featured some of the greatest mavericks of my time – add all our caps together and Carlton Palmer and David Batty got more, and I'm not having a go at them.

'Mavericks' like Terry can't be coached. They just know how to play the game. In our time, there were players in the Midlands who never got a sniff at international level because nobody came to watch them. I was talking recently with Dennis Mortimer and he reminded me that Aston Villa won the European Cup without a single international in their team.

At one stage the national team consisted totally of Liverpool and Manchester United players. Stoke manager Tony Waddington told me that I would get into a world eleven before I got into the England team. In the end I got capped because of media pressure – Don Revie didn't want to pick me.

It took a lot of foreigners to come over and save our game because they do things that most of our players can't.

I share Terry's frustration about the situation that England are stuck in now. Gareth Southgate is reluctant to play Jack Grealish, even though he should be 100 per cent the first name on the teamsheet, because he doesn't fit into the way he wants to play.

*****

I WAS the ultimate showman. My attitude was why beat a defender when you can torture him and entertain the public as well?

The 'experts' labelled me as a winger or an attacking midfielder. I wasn't either. I was the freest of spirits and needed to have a free role to show what I could do. That was a fight I lost with most of the managers that I played for.

Football is a game of skill and entertainment. I wanted to use my talent to help our team win matches and to give the fans something to remember. It didn't matter whether I was playing against a Fourth Division team or the best defenders in the world, I said 'gimme the ball' and backed myself against anyone.

People still say: "Do you remember when you did that. . . ?" They're talk about unusual things that I did on a football field 40 odd years ago – the things that got me into shed loads of trouble with managers who thought I was taking the piss.

You can't have it both ways. Either you allow players to show their talent on a football pitch or you don't. Cristiano Ronaldo, Lionel Messi, Diego Maradona and others have been brilliant because managers encouraged them to do their thing. You never saw these superstars chasing back too much to help their defence.

I'll sum it up in an exchange that I had with Saints manager Lawrie McMenemy. I was sat in the dressing room ready for kick off when legendary former Liverpool manager Bill Shankly came in for a chat. McMenemy asked Shanks who was his favourite footballer of all time and he said Tom Finney, one of England's greats. McMenemy surprised me by pointing to me and telling Shanks that he'd seen me do things in training even the famous

Tom Finney couldn't do. Did I take that as a compliment? Yes and no. I said: "So why don't you give me the freedom to go out and do it in a game?" Many managers are the same. They enjoy watching the lads show off their skills on the training pitch during the week, then go back to Plan A on a Saturday – team shape and organisation, no room for individual flair.

I don't think many managers, coaches, players or media understand footballers unless they are a chip off the old block. They think along the same tramlines, looking for athletes to cover every inch of the pitch and give their teams defensive security. Coaching books and courses don't cover encouraging talented players to do what comes naturally. Everything follows the same tired old patterns.

Media seek out so-called 'mavericks' like me because we give them headlines. That sells newspapers or attracts people to listen to the radio, TV and online broadcasts. They know Terry Curran and others won't parrot back the same boring, politically correct nonsense that they get from everyone else. But there's a downside. Those same journalists and broadcasters are the first to kick you in the teeth and push the politically correct party line.

I wasn't a total rebel. I did a lot of things right whilst others got away with murder. I worked very hard, never missed training and put in as much sweat and toil as any of my teammates to keep myself fit. I did that because I loved the game and wanted my name on the teamsheet every Saturday. I was desperate to win. Yes, I was an individual, but also a team player.

People probably think that I was a big drinker because I liked to socialise – but I honestly wasn't. On a pre-season tour with Nottingham Forest, a few of us, including me and new signing Kenny Burns, socialised together because we weren't playing in a friendly match. Burnsy, who had a bit of a reputation, knocked it back so much that he was sick which led assistant manager, Peter Taylor, to point the finger at me for leading him astray. Cloughie supported me by saying: "But he doesn't drink!" And that was generally true.

Truth was that I loved socialising with the best of them, but alcohol wasn't my thing. Yes, I had a few drinks but nine times out of ten I preferred coke. Sometimes managers encouraged me to drink more alcohol than I did! Teammates came into training on a Monday morning with hangovers, making excuses such as fake injuries. I covered up for a few in my time, but never did that myself. Same with smoking which was more common in my playing time. I played in a Forest team in which John Robertson was renowned for having a fag at half time but that never bothered me.

My vice was women. I admit it. I've not gone into detail about my adventures in this book, but it was all a natural part of my life. I married whilst I was at Nottingham Forest, with the blessing of Brian Clough and with captain John McGovern as best man, but was never suited to being tied down. I was a free spirit on the pitch and a free spirit off it. I enjoyed the company of women and, as a fit young man, was keen on sex. To me, the perfect way to relax before a game was to sneak a young lady into our hotel room whilst the boss wasn't watching. Then, after the match was over, women were the perfect way to unwind on a Saturday night.

Being a womaniser caused me problems– notably at Sheffield United when I returned home one day to find my wife and my new live-in girlfriend together – but I don't regret it. I've got great memories and I never meant any harm. Women, in my experience, are just as keen, or even more keen, on sex than men. They didn't kiss and tell and neither did I, so nobody got hurt.

Vice two is betting. I've always enjoyed a flutter. Cloughie was the first manager to take me to task whilst I was at Forest. I was having a few problems settling into the club and was quite lonely. I needed something to recreate the excitement of playing football during the week. I liked to go into William Hill after training and put £100 or so on the horses. I wasn't the only footballer in the world with time on his hands who did that.

Usually, I lost, including one bizarre night when I put £200 on England to win in Czechoslovakia and the game was abandoned after a few minutes! That wasn't a problem, because I knew I could make the money back, but when my Mum found a £4,000 betting slip in my pocket it got more serious. I'd taken my cut from the transfer to Forest and put it on a horse during a mad moment. And, you guessed it, it lost!

Mum then reported the incident to the boss who gave me sensible advice. Liking the odd wager himself, he wasn't too hard on me, but said there was no such thing as a poor bookmaker!

140

However clever I thought I was, I would always lose in the end. Of course, I've carried on betting and proved Cloughie right. But I've done it knowing the score and without it wrecking my life or anyone else's. So, yeah, hands up I'm a gambler but, like the women, I've enjoyed it.

Horse racing is another way of relaxing before kick off. Some footballers love to psyche themselves up. They get into the dressing room well before they are told to and go through their rituals to get ready for the game. I didn't need to do that. Come 3pm I was ready and up for it, whether it was a pre-season friendly or a cup final. I remember going into dressing rooms about 2.45pm when the manager said 'no later than 2.30pm'. I would say 'don't worry, just gimme the ball'. Huddersfield manager, Mick Buxton, had to get me off the bus at Hull City where I was sat with one of my mates 'fat man' Tony Kelly shouting Pebbles to victory in a horse race.

People are different. The way I prepared for a football match wasn't the same as others. I never spent time taking on board lots of information about my opponents – if they're being honest, not many lads do. They'll nod in the right place and say 'yes, boss' but their mind is usually somewhere else. Then they'd say: "Well, that was a load of crap'. Managers told me off for 'not listening to them'. I said: "I've listened to every word you've said, I just don't agree with you!'

It was the same thing at most clubs that I played for. I'm a huge fan of Howard Kendall, but remember listening on the way to Old Trafford to the lads being told how great all the Manchester United players were. My reply was to go through some of our squad – all tremendous players – and say 'come on lads, let's have a go at them'. And we did – we got a well earned 1-1 draw in a brilliant game of football. Not long afterwards it was Everton who were looked upon as the best team in the land and no doubt our opponents started putting us on a pedestal.

It was even more funny listening to Huddersfield Town manager, Mick Buxton, bigging up modest Second Division opponents and I still think that is self defeating. You don't get anywhere telling players that the opposition are better than you. It was the opposite at Forest where Cloughie told some players that they were better than they were! The result was when they fully trusted the manager, they began to believe that they would never lose a football match.

Being different isn't easy – it made me a target on the football field and that got me into trouble. I was sent off about six times in my professional career and got a fair few bookings. But not many were for a foul.

I got myself into a running battle with the referee. Everyone knew the opposition's hard men paid special attention to talented players. Back then, for some reason, officials had an unofficial totting up procedure before handing out yellow or red cards.

You hardly ever saw a player booked in the first few minutes of a match or for their first foul. This meant that they knew they could get away with just about anything early on. I got scythed to the floor and asked the referee 'what are you going to do about it?'

His typical reply was: 'it was his first foul'.

That set me ticking. A few minutes later, another defender came in with a brutal challenge and I got the same rubbish from the ref.

I told him 'that's the second tackle'.

And he replied 'yes, but it's the player's first'.

When the original defender fouled me again, I was mad. He got a yellow card whilst I often talked myself into the book for saying sarcastically 'was that his first tackle, ref?' You might think I was being petty, but you weren't on the receiving end of those tackles. I can hardly walk now and being kicked up in the air every Saturday afternoon didn't help! Today referees often give forwards more protection by judging tackles on their merits. You see cards produced earlier in games and they can be red if sufficiently bad. But, back in the day, talented players suffered.

How often have you heard the phrase 'it's going to take a piece of magic to win this game'? But when a player tries something out of the ordinary, they are much more likely to get a bollocking than a thumbs up, except, of course from Cloughie!

I got myself into hot water when my tricks went right, let alone when they went wrong. The steel city derbies against Sheffield United in the 1979/80 provided a couple of examples.

What I did on Boxing Day wasn't planned but came about partly as a result of all the pre-match talk. We were strolling towards our 4-0 victory when I came over to take a corner at the Leppings Lane end in front of disappointed Blades fans. I spread myself out on the turf like I was on a sunbed before picking myself up and taking the corner.

I did that to get a reaction from both sets of fans. I was saying that beating Sheffield United was a stroll in the park. I knew that would give the Wednesday fans a good laugh and tell Blades not to treat us like big brother. Let's face it, we well and truly put them back in their place. It's easier to do that kind of thing when you're winning 4-0 but would I have done it if we were only one or two up? Yes, I would!

Although delighted with the result and my contribution, Jack was angry about my antics in the corner. He was brought up under Don Revie who was very superstitious – such as getting off the coach and walking a few hundred yards to the ground. Jack didn't want his teams to do anything to give our opponents ammunition when we met again.

I understood his point of view. If that happened to us, we'd have pinned a photo of me showboating onto the dressing room wall as extra motivation to get revenge. But that didn't worry me. I went to Bramall Lane on Easter Saturday to thrash them again, if possible.

What Owls fans probably don't realise is how close I got to getting into more trouble with Big Jack because of again doing it 'my way'. Owls striker Andy McCulloch, who was on the sidelines that day through injury, knows the truth.

Nothing was going right, either for me or for Wednesday as The Blades scored the first goal and held their lead until deep into the second half. With both teams whacking it long and kicking lumps out of each other, chances were very rare as we looked for an equaliser.

When I picked up the ball tight to the byline, there wasn't much on. Two Blades defenders were breathing down my neck and it would have been easier to make a short pass to get myself out of trouble or to lump the ball into the crowded penalty area.

Instead I turned back infield and held onto possession. My pace took me away from my markers, then two more Blades players. All the time I was scanning, knowing exactly where the goal was. Then I turned inside and found room for a shot. I caught it perfectly with my right foot from about 20 yards and it whistled into the corner of the net. It was one of those perfect moments.

Everything happened exactly how I'd envisioned it and Owls fans in a crowd of more than 46,000 went mad. People still talk about that goal to this day.

But Andy's comment told me what the manager thought. "He was going ballistic," he said, fighting to hold back his laughter. Big Jack didn't want to see me holding onto the ball and taking on Blades defenders – he wanted me to play the ball to David Grant or loft it for our tall strikers to challenge for it in the penalty area.

Andy said Jack was literally screaming for me to pass the ball – what the f--- was I doing taking the ball away from their goal! Knowing Jack, I could see his anger and the look on his face changing when he saw the ball nestling in the back of United's net.

If I hadn't scored, I'd have been guaranteed a huge bollocking instead of the cheers when I walked off the pitch. That was Jack Charlton and professional football back in 1980 but I'm not having a go at him. A lot of managers think the same way decades later.

When a player does a trick or a piece of magic in a junior or amateur game, the reaction from everyone is 'wow, can you do that again?' But in a professional match the reaction is totally different. Like Big Jack, managers and coaches think what would have happened if I'd lost that ball. Could I have put our team under pressure by conceding possession and allowing United to counterattack? Think about it. It's more likely that a piece of magic will open up the opposition defence and lead to a goal than the ball ending up in our net. But most managers think safety first.

I can't count the times I got myself into trouble for trying something different. Sheffield Wednesday fans still remember incidents from otherwise boring football matches without the team ever being put at a disadvantage. The Wednesday lads loved the way that I wound Big Jack up, partly because they daren't do it themselves. I told them about the next game and what I was going to do and my teammates dared me to do it.

I thought for a couple of weeks about going round a goalkeeper and, instead of blasting the ball straight into the net, stopping the ball on the goal line, dropping onto my hands and knees and heading the ball in. I don't think anyone in the Wednesday team thought that I would ever do it.

The time came in a clash with one of my old clubs Derby County at Hillsborough. It was an important Second Division match with us still in with a reasonable chance of promotion and there was a big crowd there for what is almost a local derby. Predictably the game was tight and still 0-0 when my big moment came.

One of the lads played me through and I got past a couple of players and the goalkeeper at the Leppings Lane end. There was nobody anywhere near me, so I carried out my plan. When I nodded the ball into the empty net, I was looking to see where Big Jack was, rather than checking that the goal had been given.

I saw him out of the corner of my eye, running up the touchline, his face red with anger. Then he stopped and turned round to curse as I got up to celebrate, only to realise that the referee had disallowed the goal because another player was offside.

The lads knew what the score would be when we went off at half time, telling me that this was going to be fun. Jack set about me saying "If you do that again I'll f------ knock your head off." The lads behind Jack laughed as I took the full force of Jack's spitting, screaming and shouting. Yet, when it all calmed down and we were in the showers after the final whistle, the lads had tears of laughter in their eyes. They respected me because I had the balls to stand up to people in days when players were often frightened to death of managers.

Did I do anything to stop Wednesday from winning? No. I would never have done that. Had there been a defender or the goalkeeper snapping at my heels, I would have kicked the ball into the net like anybody else. But I had the freedom of Hillsborough to do what I wanted and I gave everyone who watched it something to remember.

Some people call me big headed. I understand that. But I'm honestly not. I come from a family of eight in a small Yorkshire town and I'm as down to earth as you will ever get. But I thought then and I still think now that football is a beautiful game won by outstanding skill, not by rolling your sleeves up and going to war.

Another way I showboated, brought a few smiles to people's faces and made a point at Wednesday, was through my goal celebrations. I've already written about sliding to my knees in front of the empty terraces at Hillsborough, but I also had some fun during a home game against Bristol Rovers.

This was during a time when the 'boring farts' at the Football Association were seeking to stop some of the more exuberant goal celebrations. To the stuffed shirts in Lancaster Gate the sight of grown men getting up close and personal with each other for a few seconds was just too much to bear. They hated all the hugging and kissing and preferred a good old gentleman's handshake.

This, to me, was total nonsense and, worse still, took some of the fun out of the game. Supporters do crazy things when their team scores and so do footballers. It's natural, it's part of the appeal of the game. Scoring a goal is the hardest and most important part of a football match and if you can't celebrate that we might as well all give up.

Anyway, I had my special way of taking the piss out of the FA's spoil sports. I told Ian Mellor what would happen if I scored but I'm not sure how many of my teammates believed me. There were a few more normal celebrations as Andy McCulloch helped himself to a couple of goals and Mark Smith got one, too; but it was mine that Wednesday fans remember as I ran back to the centre circle and did a gentlemanly bow to all four sides of Hillsborough to show them what one of the FA's approved celebrations looked like!

Cloughie and Howard Kendall encouraged me to get hold of the ball and run with it when I could, rather than thinking what might happen if I lost possession. McMenemy was the opposite. One miserable afternoon at Elland Road we were getting beat 4-0 in front of a raucous home crowd. There's always a great atmosphere at Leeds, especially when they are giving their opponents a roasting and this was almost as one-sided as the famous game when Bremner and Giles and co. whipped Saints 7-0.

I was substitute and had been watching Tony Currie give us a football lesson when McMenemy turned to me with 85 minutes gone and asked me to do something to 'change the game'. 'Bloody hell', what was he on? Four goals down with five minutes to go - Pele, Maradona, Messi and George Best rolled into one would have struggled to do that!

So instead, I had a laugh. I trapped the ball on my knee with the Leeds defender looking at me in disgust. 'Come and get it' I shouted before slipping the ball through his legs and racing away. It was an innocuous incident in a game that was already lost, but at least it raised our spirits for a short moment.

McMenemy was as pissed off as Jack Charlton. "What the hell were you doing?" he said. Or something like that.

"You told me to change the game – I did something different," I said. I reckon Cloughie would have loved it – not that his team were 4-0 down very often. He encouraged me to have a go at my marker and hit the space behind. That takes bravery and includes the risk of quickly conceding possession back to the opposition and facing a counterattack.

The way I played meant that I didn't fit into the English system. Managers could only think of either playing me wide on the flanks or as an orthodox striker. The same problem applied to one or two of the other superstars that I mentioned. When Charlie George, probably the most naturally talented lad that I ever played with, made his full England international debut he was stuck on the left wing. No wonder he only lasted an hour.

Managers and systems don't win football matches. Great players do. If you can't fit the best talents into a formation, you need to do something about it. Who would have thought that until John Robertson emerged as a world class player at Forest that a team could function with a left winger as the playmaker?

I was never afraid to stand out on a football pitch. Media reported that Frenchman, Eric Cantona, was the first player with his collar up on his shirt. It gave him an air of being the boss, someone who knew how good he was. Well, I did it years before and I didn't get any praise for it. I got a right bollocking.

What harm was I causing wanting to play with my collar up? Some players would have crumbled, but I stood up and was never going to be bullied. I was playing for Wednesday at Wimbledon and wanted to send them a message. Everyone knew that Wimbledon players were thugs and they would make you pay if you showed any fear, so I did the opposite. I was taking the experience in my stride by wearing my collar up – and I proved it by scoring.

Coaches don't help. When I was coaching, the head coach pointed at players wearing coloured boots as if they were doing something wrong. What's wrong with playing in coloured boots and why make the players feel uncomfortable? Playing with your shirt collar up and playing with coloured football boots doesn't make you play badly. Instead, it's the negativity from some managers that puts players under pressure and doesn't help their confidence.

Part of doing it 'my way' has been expressing my own opinions about football. I did it whilst I was a player and it got me into trouble with managers and I do it today as a fan and it loses me the odd friend on social media.

I have listened to the views of others on the game and I know that there is more than one way to play football. I also know that the stats stack up that players who do unpredictable things and have got touch and technique always win the major trophies. Yes, great teams are based on a top goalkeeper and a solid defence, but you need flair to unlock the door and win important games. Teams like Ajax, Liverpool and Forest from my day, who keep the ball on the floor and play with tempo, are the ones who succeed.

I don't regret doing and saying things my way – and can honestly say that I have even tried to help win football matches and make them more entertaining.

CHAPTER SIX
MANAGING AND COACHING

By GARY HURLSTONE, Goole Town striker

TERRY CURRAN signed me for Goole as one of four players who came from Bridlington. He was such a big figure in the game, a tremendous player, joining up with him was a no-brainer.

We were playing fast attacking football that second season in the Northern Premier League. I don't think Goole fans had seen anything like it. I played up front with Pete Collier and we were both prolific.

It was a great time for all of us with a good feel about the place. It's a shame that Terry's time was cut short because we thought we could go places in a very strong league with clubs who have since made it into the Football League.

As for Terry himself, he's a cracking bloke. I turned up in a tracksuit, so he bought me a Hugo Boss suit. I had it for years and told people 'Terry Curran bought me this'.

*****

CLOUGHIE famously said that he may not have been the best manager but was in the top one! As for me, I don't THINK I would have been a very good football manager, I KNOW I would.

It's partly my fault why it hasn't happened. Football is in my blood, but I fell out of love with the game and went instead into business. Altogether I was out of the sport for about 17 years.

That probably ended my best chance of getting another manager's job after working at Northern Premier League clubs, Goole Town and Mossley.

I became one of many young managers who take jobs with struggling clubs, before being dumped without getting on the bandwagon – those who go from job to job and never achieve much.

I got the Goole job in strange circumstances. After finishing professionally, I played again for Kinsley Boys and then did my mate, Martin O'Neill, a favour at Grantham when I could barely walk.

My friend Peter Brown kept on at me about joining Goole as a player and eventually I gave in. Goole were a struggling team in the Northern Premier League, a strong division one rung below the Conference.

I scored a couple of goals in my first home match at the Victoria Pleasure Grounds and also got the winner at Frickley. But the pain in my knee soon became too much and I had to pack in playing. Goole were then eight points adrift at the bottom when manager Paddy Buckley got the sack.

Chairman Chris Raywood asked me back to Goole as manager. I agreed and Pete Brown came in as my assistant. I ran the team for nothing. It even cost me money when I chipped in for scrambled egg and toast on away trips. I worked with one of the smallest budgets in our league, £750 a week, with our highest paid player, former West Ham and York striker Dale Banton, getting £50.

A deal I did with Bridlington Town owner Ken Richardson, who later went to prison after his role in burning down a stand at my first professional club Doncaster Rovers, helped to turn things round for us. They came in for one of our players and we snapped up Gary Lee, Gary Lockwood, Gary Hurlstone and Dave Travis in part exchange.

Results soon started to improve after we looked to have no chance of staying up when I took over. Travelling to Caernarfon on a Tuesday night needing a draw to maintain our Northern Premier League status, I put myself in the team because I didn't have anyone else. I missed three good chances, but it was more important that we got a 0-0 draw as beating the drop was a great start for me as a manager.

I contacted my old boss, Brian Clough, who kindly agreed to send a strong Nottingham Forest side to Goole for a pre-season friendly. We also got a good crowd for the visit of Leeds United.

I brought in more funds by selling defender Ian Sampson to Sunderland for £8,000 and Wigan manager Brian Hamilton snapped up left winger Jeremy Smith for £5,000.

We did well in the pre-season games and I told the lads that, although we didn't have a lot of money, they would enjoy their football and we would always try to win games. I knew that it was important they enjoyed training as part time players juggle the game with jobs and other responsibilities. We mixed together and Goole became a happy club, all the more so because we were winning.

I asked the chairman whether the club could afford to go up a level into the Conference and he assured me that they could. I told him I had agreed a 'bonus' with the players – no more wages but, if we got promotion, we would take them abroad for a 10-day break or a holiday in England.

What I didn't know was that, whilst I was looking after my transport café business, Chris and Pete Brown met the players and agreed to pay a bonus based on results.

The first few weeks of the season were very successful. We were top of the league, having won eight and drawn one of our first nine games. That sort of thing didn't happen at Goole.

Also, we were playing the kind of passing football that I wanted to be associated with. Crowds doubled to between 300 and 400 and everything was looking good. All this despite only using £450 a week of our budget.

Positive media attention came our way, including iconic Times reporter Brian Glanville, whom I met when I was at Forest. He had heard good things about how I was doing in my first job as a manager. We pencilled in time to meet in a couple of weeks.

Then I got an urgent phone call from Chris Raywood saying that I needed to see him at his bungalow. He cracked open a bottle of champagne, before telling me that he had bad news – the club owed the players £1,000. I asked him how when we had made about £29,000 from pre-season games and player sales and only used part of our budget. He said that the money had gone on paying bills and a bonus for every point that he had agreed with the players. He hadn't bargained for us winning so many games and this had hit him in the pocket, so he wanted me to tell the lads that we needed to get rid of some of them to reduce the wage bill. I told him that was his job. I couldn't believe all this had happened because of his mistakes.

I only lasted a couples of games after that before I walked out. I told Brian Granville I couldn't do his interview as I had left. I honestly think we could have achieved success at Goole and that may have put me in contention for a Football League job. But it wasn't to be.

My second job was a case of the right club at the wrong time. In contrast to Goole, Mossley had been a very successful side at NPL level with ambitions to go higher. But they were in a very poor state when I joined them.

Looking back, I should have listened to former Manchester United star Sammy Mcilroy who had just been Mossley's manager. He marked my card whilst I was watching a match at Altrincham. He told me the story behind them conceding fours and fives every week - they were in a big financial mess – and warned me not to touch them.

Anyway, I decided to take the job with assistant Paul Jones, the former Bolton defender, and found out the harsh truth for myself. We were immediately struggling for players as several of the better players left with Sammy and didn't have the money to pay the wages of replacements.

We lost our first game 5-2 and things never got any better. After six successive defeats, we were 3-0 down at half time in what proved to be my final game. I tried to tell our centre back that he needed to get tighter. Then Billy Whitehurst, the former Hull City striker, pinned the defender against the dressing room wall. I'm not having a go at Billy, an honest guy only wanting the best for the team. We lost 6-1 and, after what happened in the dressing room, there was no way back for me. So I offered my resignation to the chairman.

In the months after Mossley, I found out what my former Forest mate, Martin O'Neill, was talking about when I took Goole to play his Shepshed Charterhouse side.

A famous player, who had achieved so much in the game, he had written a shedload of applications for jobs without getting a single reply. He still had the letters to prove it. Luckily, he got his big break at Wycombe Wanderers, taking them into the Football League.

I applied for more jobs and got nowhere. The nearest miss was getting an interview at Northwich Victoria.

And, yes, I did apply to become manager of my club Sheffield Wednesday. In fact I did it two or three times, once when they had just gone down to the Third Division.

Some people took it as a joke that I offered to manage The Owls for nothing. It was no joke.

My relative lack of experience in management was no issue for me because I knew I could do the job. I told Dave Allen that I would work without a wage because I knew I could prove myself and earn a contact.

I could have done a better job than many Owls bosses because of my knowledge of the game, having a philosophy of how to play that would suit the players and what I took on board from some of the best managers. I would have used Cloughie's way but given it a modern twist with a high press and tempo and stressing the importance of how dangerous the opposition can be when we don't have the ball. I understand the small details of the game and have never lacked belief in my own ability.

After the long break from football, my coaching career started after my nine-year-old son Jock was approached by scouts from Leeds United and Doncaster Rovers at a tournament. Whilst at Leeds, Trevor Todd, who now works for Manchester City, asked me to do some coaching there.

Jock was offered a contract with Donny, but I went to Leeds where Trevor Potter asked me to do a coaching course and work with the club's academy. It started as two days a week and eventually became five.

I'd already been on FA coaching courses at Huddersfield Town and Sheffield United and wasn't impressed. I got my UEFA 'B' licence but decided not to do the pro licence. Maybe I should have listened to wise heads who advised me to get through the courses, get the qualifications, then do it my way.

Much of the time was spent on channel plays. This is where full backs kick the ball long into the opposition's half into the channels and the team then pushes up to try to win the ball back - the kind of football I hated as a player. It's safety-first football when managers aren't confident that they can play out from defence and pass it.

The other tactic that they concentrated on was switching play from one side of the pitch to the other. This looks good and gets applause from the crowd when a defender or midfielder plays a 30 or 40-yard ball to the opposite flank. But you don't often get anything positive out of it. Players tend to occupy the area near the ball. The long crossfield pass is almost always played in the air and the time it takes to reach its target allows the opposition to read it and regain possession. There's also the problem of players having to race across the field to support. Otherwise, you can be outnumbered and vulnerable to a counterattack. I'm not saying never play a crossfield ball – it can be a good tactic when the opposition is short of players on the opposite flank. But only do it when things are in your favour.

Look at how great midfielders, Iniesta and Xavi, played for Spain and Barcelona. They kept possession and played in triangles, looking for angles and then releasing the killer ball forward when it was on. They didn't use up valuable energy dashing from one side of the pitch to the other.

Leeds suited me as we were living at Garforth, but my priority was my son and how he was progressing. His mum, who took him to Doncaster, said that they spent more time sitting on the floor than being coached.

When I took a look for myself, John Bilton, who had worked previously with Howard Wilkinson, suggested that I switch to Donny. I was only in the development section at Leeds and he said that they could get me through my badges and give me any age group I wanted from the under 9s to the under 16s. The usual system was that coaches swapped age groups at the end of the season. I wasn't interested in that. I asked to work with Jock's age group all the way through to ensure that they were coached properly. John agreed and I did so for the next couple of years.

John then went to Fenerbahce in Turkey and his successor, Mick Tarmey, said that a different coach would take over Jock's group at the end of the season. I bit my tongue and stayed a year longer than I expected. Altogether I spent more than three seasons coaching at Donny during two spells.

First team managers vary in the interest that they take in the youngsters. When Darren Ferguson was manager of Donny, he followed in the footsteps of Sir Alex who knew all the young players at Manchester United. I was taking the under 14s when Darren came to watch all the age groups training. He was with me for about 20 minutes, longer than anyone else.

He broke off to speak on the phone with his famous father who passed on his best wishes after remembering me as a player. Darren said that he liked the way I was training the youngsters and how the session was going. He suggested that I work with the under 18s at Donny, but this was never passed on to me.

I taught my age group how to play out from the back. Parents were supportive when we won, but our tactics were all wrong when we lost. Fortunately, we only lost half-a-dozen games in three seasons.

I wanted to win, but also to improve players and give them the chance to play the right way. I taught defenders how to open up their bodies to want to receive the ball from the goalkeeper. Watch a lot of professionals and you see the opposite. Defenders show from their body shape they don't want the ball, forcing the goalkeeper to kick it long and probably lose possession.

Defenders who open up their bodies have two choices – under pressure, they can play the ball back to the goalkeeper; given time and space, they can pass it forward. Dribbling out of defence is even more dangerous. Players have to learn about staying calm under pressure and to make good, early decisions. If they can do this and retain the ball, space opens up to create chances at the other end of the pitch. Beating the opposition's press leaves them shorter in defence.

This isn't easy for young footballers – and mistakes are inevitable. Sometimes they lose the ball and give goals away. That's when parents said that we were getting it wrong. But, given time and practice, the Donny youngsters got better and made fewer mistakes.

We didn't have the very best young players. In the Yorkshire area, they are snapped up by elite clubs, such as Manchester United and Manchester City with Leeds, Sheffield United and Wednesday getting next pick. Clubs like Donny live off scraps as most local youngsters go to bigger clubs if they get the chance.

I found the same problem working in academies as I did as a professional footballer – managers asked my honest opinion but didn't like it when I disagreed.

I didn't like how they judged players. Some youngsters develop physically quicker than others. This leads academies to have a false opinion. The lad bangs in lots of goals against opponents half his size and they think he is a future star. But, when others catch up, this proves to be untrue.

I looked for youngsters with better technical ability. Many think their job is to develop athletes – as you see at first team level in the modern game – rather than footballers. That was never my way.

After my first spell at Donny, I went to Barnsley as Ronnie Branson and Mark Burton gave me the chance to get more coaching badges. I think that they knew the weaknesses of the courses as much as I did, but told me that I needed to do them to progress my career. I took over the under 12s who were a poor bunch, apart from three or four players.

Barnsley are in much the same league as Doncaster when it comes to snapping up young footballers – having second choice after the big boys have grabbed the best. I worked with Gary Walsh and asked who had signed some of the lads. This told me that some staff didn't know much about the game.

My judgement on how bad we were was highlighted when we got beaten 16-1 by Manchester City. Ronnie, who always rang me afterwards, told me not to worry about the result. I said that I never worried about anything in my life! Things didn't get any better against Newcastle as we lost by the same massive scoreline. That was 32 goals conceded in two games!

Players came to Barnsley in eight-week blocks, giving us a chance to sign them or let them go. This enabled me to mix up the side by bringing trialists. Getting beaten 3-1 by Sunderland was a step in the right direction after the hammerings.

We showed how far we had come when we played Manchester United. It was an unusual arrangement because we both fielded two sides playing short periods. The idea was to pick and mix the better and weaker lads, but I didn't think that was in the best interests of my players. I picked one strong team, which I took charge of, and Gary looked after the weaker lads. This wasn't for personal benefit. The best way for young players to improve, in my view, was to get as much game time as possible with lads of the same standard.

My team produced a really good performance to beat United 7-4. You could see what an achievement this was because some of the United lads were crying on the pitch as they weren't used to losing. I even had a phone call from Ronnie Branson congratulating the team as they never got a positive result against United. Unsurprisingly, Gary's side got trounced and we lost overall but I was happy with the way things had gone, even if it didn't fit with the club's policy.

I wasn't into equal opportunities when it came to ability. We probably only had two or three lads in our group with the talent to push on and become better players. You only have to ask the parents what reaction they get from the young players about the team performance and their teammates after the game.

The next fall out I had at Barnsley though proved terminal. I fell foul of the system trying to put out my best side for a game against Sheffield United. Joe Webster, a technically good player who had been to St George's Park for England to look out, had been injured during the week. Scott Rogan, who oversaw the under 9s and under 12s, told me not to play him and this was confirmed as club policy by Ronnie. But, after Joe had trained both on the Friday and Saturday morning, I stuck to my guns and put him in my starting line up on the Sunday.

The arguments continued when I was pulled into the office afterwards where Mark Burton, Ronnie's assistant, again talked about club policy. That was when I told them to stick their club up their arse.

Altogether I spent six years coaching in academy football. I enjoyed being back in the game and working with young players. But I don't miss it now. I quit to watch my son Jock who was with Grimsby Town.

The experience gave me insight into what we are doing with our young players in this country and I have problems with our academy system at the lower level.

I wouldn't scrap it, but I think it should be changed. In my view, we are not helping young players by coaching them too early in their development. I would prefer to see the age groups continue but the coaches step aside until they reach the age of 14.

Allow the lads to go out there and enjoy playing. Allow them to express themselves without getting too worried about results

Then when the coaches come in, they can start teaching them the game and improve them very quickly.

Also some coaches – at least at the level I worked at – aren't the best. They are more like gym teachers than professional football coaches. I'm not being negative for the sake of it, but you can't teach others about the game when you don't know much about it yourself.

They are tied into a system where they spend more time on a computer inputting data than on the field. Data can be a very useful tool. But a lot of box ticking and unnecessary nonsense goes on such as awarding each player a regular mark out of ten. Some getting eights and nines have no chance of making it in the game. The need for coaches to 'look good' means that they sometimes over rate the players and agree with whatever their academy bosses say.

The aims of the academies seemed to be to bring one player through, but that's not enough in my opinion. Coaches then concentrate on their favourite players at the expense of the others. If that's the limit of their ambitions, is it really worth the lower league clubs running academies? Some clubs instead bring in lads who get released by the bigger clubs further down the line at 16 or 17. I would rather see academies change than go down this route.

Young players need better continuity. The same coach should look after them through the age groups rather than changing every year. Coaches should also share the same ideas on how the game should be played. But this is very difficult when clubs are constantly chopping and changing first team managers.

My honest opinion from what I saw and experienced is that we are still not doing our youngsters justice at this level and that leads to many being disappointed.

PART THREE
MODERN DAY FOOTBALL

AS a footballer supposedly with no brains and no college education, I often stuck my neck out over what was coming next in football.

When playing for Sheffield Wednesday I had my own weekly column in the Sheffield Star where I predicted things that others didn't see happening. And, of course, I got a lot of stick from people who thought I was off my head.

I wrote about many more foreign players, managers and coaches coming into the English game. In 2021, we take all those things for granted. I wrote about the terraces being replaced by all-seater stadiums. That also happened long ago as one by one everyone followed in the footsteps of Jimmy Hill and Coventry City.

And whilst the football world was taking in the shock of Trevor Francis becoming the first million-pound footballer, I forecast transfers with £10m and upwards changing hands. The journalist who helped with my article looked at me as if I'd completely lost it.

You see, I've never been 'old school' in that sense. I've always looked forward because in football, as in life itself, nothing stands still. And I don't slag off modern football just because I played in different times. Instead, I'll be honest and tell you the things that I like and those that I don't.

The arrival of foreign players and now more foreign coaches has been positive for our game, in my view, and is now helping to improve the England national team.

I played in an international tournament in Spain whilst at Derby. Playing against Atletico Madrid, Valencia and River Plate was great because I saw at first hand the skills of World Cup winners, like Mario Kempes and Leopoldo Luque. I could see their technique and that they were playing with the style I liked and being encouraged by their managers and coaches to do so.

In contrast, our football was getting boring before Ossie Ardiles and Ricardo Villa burst onto the scene at Tottenham. As the game was getting more technical overseas, our managers and coaches were going down the opposite route. They focused more and more on the physical, athletic side.

Our football became more about power than natural talent. We have always produced technical players, including Alan Hudson, Tony Currie, Stan Bowles, Charlie George, Frank Worthington, Simon Stainrod and Dave Thomas, but we generally didn't pick them at international level. We will never know what would have happened to England had we given the better technical players their chance – but those mistakes from the 1970s, when we failed to qualify for two World Cups, have been repeated many times over since.

The way that we played in my day meant those clubs, who kept true to their principles and played on the floor, such as Liverpool and Forest, swept all before them.

Foreign players then came in – but not ones who could take our game forward. We tended to bring in players from Sweden, Norway and sometimes Denmark, who had often been coached by English managers.

I got a glimpse of what might have been from a couple of foreign players that I played with who made an impact upon me. At Saints, we had Yugoslavian right back Ivan Golac, who was physically fit, technically good and an intelligent footballer. Wednesday signed Ante Mirocevic, originally from Montenegro, who won international caps for Yugoslavia. He summed up the problems that the technical players faced in the British game; being our most naturally talented player in the Second Division but he was being brought down to our level by the style of football.

I spent time with Ivan and Ante, inviting them to my house and seeing them in their rented accommodation and discovered a different football culture. They were surprised that some of the British players drunk a lot of alcohol and didn't look after their bodies and talked about the importance of nutrition and eating properly. Again, these are things that we now almost take for granted in the modern game where it's the minority who go drinking. In my day, I'd say this was one of the reasons that we used to do a lot of running on a Monday at some clubs – to run off the excesses of Saturday and Sunday nights.

It was the introduction of the Premier League in 1992 that rekindled my interest in the game and started to take us forward. Football was in danger of dying with even some of the biggest clubs in the land struggling to attract crowds when the breakaway league came in like a breath of fresh air and Sky TV presented it to the public in a positive and new way.

This was also when the superstar foreigners began to come to England as well as more top managers and coaches.

A great example was Arsene Wenger who did so much to change and modernise Arsenal from a side better known for their defensive strength. And he did it very cleverly. Among his best signings were players who had previously struggled to fulfil their full potential but became legends in world football when under the wing of a top coach whose philosophy suited their game.

Thierry Henry had played wide on the left in France's World Cup winning side in 1998. Wenger gave him more freedom up front and suddenly we saw a great talent emerge, one of the best in the game. And it was a similar story with Patrick Vieira and Dennis Bergkamp, who were both stifled by defensive football in Italy, but flourished in Wenger's free flowing side.

Altogether, the number of foreign stars who came to England is too great to mention, but players such as Ruud van Nistelroy, Jaap Stam, Cristiano Ronaldo and Eric Cantona at Manchester United, were great for our game.

On the managerial side, British managers became left behind. Howard Wilkinson being the last Englishman to win the title way back in the last season of the First Division in 1992.

The notable exception was Sir Alex Ferguson, who did a great job for Manchester United as they dominated the topflight during his time at Old Trafford. But, generally, successful managers have come from abroad, improving the technical side of club football.

It has taken a long while for this to filter through to the England team and I was disappointed that Glenn Hoddle followed the trend when he was in charge. Having had to battle to get into the England team himself, despite being one of the most technical players of his own generation, I expected him to give Paul Gascoigne and Matt Le Tissier more opportunities.

England fell a long way behind other countries in Europe because of our coaching and the way that we play. Germany and France both won tournaments with technical players and Holland, known for their technical side, were arguably the best team never to win the World Cup on two occasions in 1974 and 1978.

But Spain is the success story that I would highlight. In my time, their football was as brutal as Argentina's, but they were transformed when the great Johan Cruyff brought his total football from Holland. I think it was his vision and brilliance, taken further by Pep Guardiola and then Vicente del Bosque, that led them to become one of the outstanding teams at international level.

Many have argued that the influx of foreign managers and players has held back the English players, but now we are seeing this isn't true.

We have always produced good players but the young stars who have come through today are exceptional. I'm referring to Jack Grealish, Phil Foden, Mason Mount, John Stones, Jude Bellingham, Jadon Sancho, Mason Greenwood, James Maddison, Ben White, Raheem Sterling, Reece James and Callum Hudson-Odoi in particular.

I honestly think that we have the talent to win an international competition, but I still don't think we have the manager. Of course, I'm willing to be proved wrong and hope that when you read this Gareth Southgate will have led us to glory in the Euros.

I credit Southgate to a certain extent for adapting his style of play, so we play out from the back and try to keep the ball. But he is too cautious in my view. I am very aware of the defensive side of the game needing to be right, but I'll ask this: where has being cautious got us in the past? To succeed at the highest level, you must take risks instead of being afraid to lose.

Southgate, like his predecessors, has fallen into the trap of picking 'safe' players that he thinks he can trust, rather than giving the most technically gifted their head. I've been saying publicly for three or four years that Jack Grealish is a top, top player, but Southgate has been reluctant to pick him. We won't win anything, in my opinion, until we make our most technically gifted players the first names on the teamsheet.

We also still need to get a better tempo to our game and I've been disappointed in seeing Southgate use two defensive midfielders, even against modest opponents. To me, this means that you don't trust the back line. We need to pick defenders who are not only good on the ball and able to bring it out, but who are also top class at defending. Then you can release midfield players to get further forward and inject more pace into the side.

Harry Maguire's injury before the Euros was a big blow in my opinion because I rate him and John Stones as central defenders who are as good as anyone on the ball. I've backed Stones throughout the time that he has been criticised and I know he has had problems off the field. But the way that Pep Guardiola reintegrated him into the Manchester City side last season, despite signing a couple of high-class defenders, shows his quality. I have also watched young Ben White, at Leeds and Brighton, and am very impressed. He is both a good defender and passes the ball intelligently and with tempo.

Hand on heart, I've never thought that we could win a tournament with Southgate in charge. Our run to the semi finals of the World Cup in Russia in 2018 flattered to deceive. We had a very easy group stage, followed by games with Columbia and Sweden. We are still second best when we come up against top sides such as France, Spain, Germany and Italy.

None of us knows for sure whether football will fully return to 'normal' in the 2021/22 season after the strange events of last season and the end to the 2019/20 campaign.

But some things are within our control and I'd like to see changes.

I've never supported footballers taking the knee before kick off and want to see it stop. To be honest, it has caused me to turn off the TV because this is not what the game of football is all about.

Of course, black lives matter. All lives matter! But I don't support the Black Lives Matter movement and I can't stand the politically correct rubbish that we get from the BBC and Sky, in particular.

If I was playing football now, I'd stand whilst all the other players were kneeling. I mean it! I wouldn't care what players, managers, or the media say about it, I never have. Kneeling indicates that you have done wrong. And I haven't. I did my research when it started and found out that Black Lives Matter is a deeply political campaign. I honestly don't think they care at all about black people.

What has happened since football has returned has caused more division, not less. I'm not on my own in what I say, but many are too scared to make their views known because they know that they will be instantly shot down. That doesn't bother me.

We've made a lot of progress on racism, both on and off the football field since I played. Yes, there was much abuse aimed at black players during the 1970s and 1980s and that needed to change. But don't get the idea that it was all one way. Nobody enjoyed the banter of rival football fans more than I did, but sometimes it does become very abusive. I was almost always a target for away fans. They called me every name under the sun. But I never complained about it. It motivated me even more and the best way to shut them up is to win.

Abuse still happens – it always will. But generally, attitudes have changed. I'm not saying that everything is perfect, but the political correctness we are subjected to now is doing more harm than good. It's putting people off football when there is so much confusion about where the game is heading.

I want to see full football grounds again, week in week out, but seeing the game played behind closed doors has got me thinking. I remember one football official – and I won't name him – say shortly after the Premier League came into existence that the leading clubs in the land didn't need fans in their grounds. Dave Whelan, former chairman of Wigan Athletic and a guy I admire for his contribution to football, later said the same thing.

I'm not saying that the fans will never return in their numbers. I'm sure they will. But I do think the 'new normal' of football behind closed doors has suited the elite clubs – and could be a feature of the sport in the future.

Particularly in the March 2020 lockdown, it felt like football fans were being conditioned for the future. Without getting off our sofas, driving miles and miles and getting freezing cold, you and I were able to view more football than ever before.

At one stage, there was a match on at 6pm and another at 8pm, several nights of the week. We even had talk of top matches that weren't being televised being available on pay per view at prices of up to £15. Thankfully, that got shot down.

It disappoints me that working class people are having the game taken away from them. They can't afford to go to grounds but instead are being asked to pay high prices to watch the sport on TV.

Real football fans know the difference between football in front of a big passionate crowd and behind closed doors. Anyone who has played at a reasonable level knows what it's like to have the support of a crowd. It makes some freeze – I get that. But, for me, it's one of the best things about the sport. Hearing that roar makes you try even harder to please them and do your best for the team. And I think it's the same for the supporters too. I'm sure that we get far more from watching a game for real in the ground and being part of that atmosphere than sitting in front of a TV.

I watched a lot of matches on Sky before I packed in my subscription and there was something missing. Everyone seemed to be going through the motions, like watching rock stars miming instead of singing and playing their instruments. I could take it or leave it – more and more times I left it!

It wasn't the same spectacle that you and I have grown to love over the years. We were told fans are the most important people in football, well, they haven't been treated that way! Instead, they have been prevented for more than a year from watching their teams live at the ground.

In my opinion, elite clubs won't be satisfied until they have got all of the broadcasting deals in their own hands. They will walk away from Sky because they see an even more lucrative future controlling how the fans watch their games.

This doesn't work for clubs lower down the pecking order, but that doesn't bother the top clubs. The thinking behind Liverpool and Manchester United's so-called Big Picture proposal, rejected by the rest of the Premier League, was to hand down a short-term fix for the lower leagues in return for breaking further away. Imagine how many TV packages the so-called Super Six - Liverpool, United, City, Chelsea, Arsenal and Spurs - could sell around the world. But what good does that do for the smaller teams in the Premier League, let alone those in the EFL and in grass roots football?

For several years before the lockdown, Premier League games were sold out with clubs maximising the number of season tickets to home fans. Manchester City, Arsenal and Spurs have also gone down the route of moving into new stadiums with higher capacities. But generally, there is a limit to how much they can increase match day revenue which, in their case, is almost peanuts, compared with the TV cash, rewards for success in the Premier League and all the various off-field deals.

The top clubs are now global brands so could sell huge numbers of 'season tickets' to watch their games on club-controlled live streams to supporters all over the world. And, unlike in a football ground, there is no limit to how many people could watch this.

All this brings me to the so-called European Super League. I think the plans that became public in April 2021 had been kept secret for years without any leaks – which is remarkable because there's usually a whistleblower. The announcement of a new breakaway league, including the big six from England and the elite in Italy and Spain, underestimated the feelings of football fans who made it loud and clear that they wouldn't stand for it. And I'm glad they did. The way that the elite clubs treated them was beyond contempt.

I'm against a European Super League, but the good news is I don't think that it will ever happen. The only benefit is for the mega rich owners of elite clubs to rake in even more money, otherwise everything is against it.

Only one team can win a league, some will finish mid-table, another will be last. How do you think fans of Manchester United or Liverpool would stomach their team finishing fifth or sixth? They expect to win league titles or cup competitions, season in and season out. I think that fans would soon get very fed up if their team weren't competing for the title.

The disruption that a Super League would cause to all the main leagues in Europe would be disastrous. We wouldn't want to be watching the Premier League minus six top sides and the Italian and Spanish leagues would also be badly hit. Spanish giants Real Madrid and Barcelona, who have the advantages of a tax loophole and a better climate, would be the only clubs to benefit, in my view.

On the other hand, football, as a national game, needs to realise that the billionaires who run our elite clubs, don't care about much else besides making money. They are used to getting their own way and one embarrassing setback won't mean that they will give up on the idea easily.

I can see why, from their selfish point of view, that they want to breakaway. The Premier League is a very attractive league and generates big audiences throughout the world. But there are limitations extending its worldwide appeal, which is what they want to do. People will tune in across the globe to watch the biggest clubs playing each other. A match between Manchester United and Liverpool is commercially attractive in many countries. But you can't generate the same interest for matches involving smaller, lesser-known clubs who park the bus. A TV audience is much more likely to switch off than fans who walk out of a ground.

What we love about the English game is where Wimbledon and Bournemouth can come from nowhere into the topflight and Leicester City perform near miracles by winning the Premier League and FA Cup, but it is not good news for the billionaires. They don't want the smaller clubs, who generate less TV interest and less income, at the same table.

The real challenge for football in my view is to make itself more watchable and more entertaining and you can't do that by changing rules or the way that leagues are organised.

It can only come from changing attitudes and improving the game. Nobody learns anything when the weaker teams park the bus and try to keep the score down. It does nothing for the players or for the fans, either in the ground or watching media. Instead, people switch off and that reduces the game's commercial appeal. This is a big issue for me. I believe that the way to take the game forward is to be more positive, rather than concentrating on getting ten players behind the ball. Even the very best players sometimes make mistakes when they are put under pressure. We also need to do something to persuade players to stop diving. That's another thing which is turning a lot of potential viewers away from the game.

Here's another must – scrap VAR! Scrap it completely, apart from goal line technology. The excitement of the game has also been reduced by the way VAR is being used in this country. It's not the fault of the technology – it's the people making the decisions. They're taking too long to make their minds up and still getting things wrong.

When players and fans aren't celebrating, in case a goal is overturned, we've got a problem. The joy of scoring and celebrating a goal is one of the most important parts of football. Instead, in the last couple of seasons we have seen the farce of the game being stopped, perhaps even after the ball has gone up the other end of the pitch and a decision being taken about what happened before. This can then take two, three or even five minutes before it's made.

Imagine Geoff Hurst racing clear, the fans starting to spill onto the pitch and the commentator saying, 'they think it's all over – hold on, they're having a review!' Sorry, it just doesn't work. It's taking too much of what is good away from the game to make hair-splitting decisions.

The priority was to get goal line decisions right. Was the ball over the line or not? That's black or white and the technology does the job. Other decisions should be left to the referee and his team. There's no reason why they get offside decisions wrong. When someone is half a yard offside, they can be spotted easily. Nobody wants to see the game brought back and a key decision made because a forward's toe or arm was offside.

Other decisions are a question of interpretation. We can come to different conclusions on issues such as handball and penalties even after watching several replays. In this case, we are better off going with what the officials saw at the time. Give them back the power to make all the decisions, but make them more accountable. We know that there have been examples of dodgy refs. where it has come out publicly afterwards that they have been bribed. Providing fans know the officials are straight, they can live with the decisions which they make and we can all get back to enjoying the sport as much as we used to.

Another part of the 'new normal' is the way that women's football is now being pushed. We have just had the announcement that matches in the Women's Super League are to be broadcast live on BBC TV from next season and I've got mixed feelings.

Some pundits don't like women's football but say the right things to keep their jobs. I have no axe to grind because I do like the women's game and I get the mickey taken out of me by my friends for saying so. I'd go as far as to say that some of the female players are more gifted technically than the males. Among the best that I have seen are three former England players – Karen Carney, Alex Scott and Eniola Aluko, who all impressed me with their natural ability. Unfortunately, our national side is now struggling since players like them hung up their boots.

The problem is that women's football is being promoted for politically correct reasons, rather than allowing it to grow at its own pace. I don't think the product is attractive enough to become as popular as the male game. This isn't a criticism. The skills are there, but the lack of power means that the games can't generate the same level of excitement.

I don't see a time when the women's game is being watched by anything like the same number of people, either in the grounds or on TV. If anything, the growth of the women's game will come at the expense of the lower league clubs in the male game. Because of this, I'm against the idea of paying women similar wages because the same amount of money will not be generated. Where is the money going to come from?

People are never going to pack out Old Trafford to watch Manchester United Women. The best way to guarantee a sizeable crowd is to play women's games before a Premier League fixture but, for obvious reasons, that's not going to happen.

Don't get me wrong, I'm not against the women's game. I intend to carry on watching and enjoying it. But you can't just thrust the 'new normal' in our face and expect people to change their habits of a lifetime.

Having played for some of the best managers of my generation, there are three who stand out for me in the Premier League.

It was no surprise to me that Manchester City regained the title in style because in Pep Guardiola they have the best of the lot. Pep has been a revelation. A product of the fantastic coaching of the late Johan Cruyff at Barcelona – another great hero of mine – he has taken the Premier League to another level with his style of football.

It's true that he has had almost unlimited funds due to Manchester City's owners. But he has been brilliant in how he has spent it. I could name a few Sir Alex signings who proved a waste of money but can't think of any that have flopped under Pep. Rather than going for superstars who may not fit into his side, he picks out players on their way up and improves them. He doesn't set transfer records but signs players in the £50m or £60m category and either gets long service from them or a good return when they move on.

His form of total passing football is the way that I like to see football played. It isn't just about keeping the ball, as some critics say, but playing with a tempo. Movement, finding angles, taking the game to their opponents, home and away and having players like Riyad Mahrez and Raheem Sterling who can go past people.

Barcelona, when they beat Sir Alex's United in the Champions League final at Wembley in 2011 and Brazil's brilliant 1970 World Cup winning side, have given me the most enjoyment in football. But City in full flow run them close.

Despite all his success, the critics were still having a go at Pep in 2019/20 when they lost the title to Liverpool. 'Where's your Plan B?' they asked as City struggled to break down defensive walls. Pep's answer would have been the same as Cloughie's: no need for a Plan B, I'll work on perfecting Plan A. And he did. City became more stable defensively and, despite not quite scoring as many as in previous seasons, made the title a one-horse race.

I thought that he would win the Champions League for City for the first time, too, but credit Chelsea – I thought they were awesome on the night and fully deserved it. So, ok, he hasn't landed the big one yet, but Pep's proved the experts wrong. They said his style of football at Barcelona and Bayern Munich wouldn't work here in the Premier League, instead it has lit up the game and won a host of trophies.

I rate Liverpool's Jurgen Klopp almost as highly. I knew from the moment that he came to Anfield things would go well for him. He is someone that players want to play for – optimistic, good with people and producing 'rock and roll' football. You can argue all you like whether his high press was new to the English game, but nobody has done it better.

It wasn't easy coming to a club who eventually waited 30 years to win back a title that the Kop once almost took for granted. But the seasons when he won the Champions League and Premier League have shown that he is up to the task. I know Klopp and Liverpool suffered a dip in form in 2020/21 but there were quite a few issues involved, not least injuries. They should have coped better but I expect Klopp and co. to come back next season.

My third favourite is Marcelo Bielsa at Leeds. What I like about him is his ability to improve players. He insisted on not spending big, but largely working with players who hadn't produced the goods at Elland Road. Like Guardiola and Klopp, he sets up his team for all-out attack, to dominate the ball and to take the game to the opposition. His team who won the Championship was great to watch, even though they didn't always convert enough of their chances. It was no surprise to me how Leeds made new friends with the way they played in the Premier League. Unlike many promoted clubs, they refused to adapt their style against the best teams. Bielsa's football is well suited to the higher level and win or lose they are always worth watching. I'd advise Leeds, though, to have a backup plan because Bielsa never seems to stay long.

All three were given time and have the respect of the owners, something rare in modern day football. In their first season, Pep scrambled fourth place in the Premier League, Klopp finished eighth and Bielsa's Leeds stumbled out of the Championship play offs after looking set for automatic promotion. I'm not saying that all managers should get more time but when you've got a good one it makes sense to stick with them.

I can now add in new Chelsea manager, Thomas Tuchel, who played a large part in their Champions League triumph. He has taken over an attacking side and given them the tactical edge when they are facing sides like Manchester City. In all three games in which he faced up to City last season, his team was the one who stopped the killer pass between the lines and the off-the-ball movement that destroys most sides. They didn't give City time and space on the ball, pressed to win the ball back in good areas and then hit opponents on the counter with blistering pace.

Tuchel's improvements at Chelsea should lead, in my opinion, to a much closer Premier League title race in 2021/22. I still see Manchester City winning it but expect Chelsea, Manchester United and Liverpool to all push them harder. I know how hard it is to retain the title and that Pep will give more thought and emphasis to try to finally land the Champions League. But I think they're the one club with the strength in depth to be able to handle both challenges.

Looking at British managers and coaches, I do like Brendan Rodgers. A key part of the revolution at Swansea, where a succession of managers have had the Swans playing the right way, he has been successful at both Liverpool and Celtic before the great job that he is doing now at Leicester City.

I think most people thought Leicester's time had come and gone after their fantastic Premier League title win in 2016. When Claudio Ranieri was sacked before the end of the following season and they were struggling in the league, it was easy to write them off as a one-off.

Yet after a couple of other managers have come and gone, Rodgers has taken them to a new and consistently high level. They'll never be as large a club as the so-called big six, but right now Leicester are competing with them football-wise and have the FA Cup to prove it. He believes in his players, doesn't fear anyone and never parks the bus. Make no mistake, he will get a top job either here or abroad.

Eddie Howe is another that I will be keeping an eye on. He's got a relegation on his CV after eventually taking Bournemouth down in 2020 but I don't think that's an issue. Bournemouth were a club nowhere near Premier League status who got propelled into that category by mega rich Russian owners. Their lifespan in the topflight was always going to be limited, rather like Brighton and Burnley who will eventually go the same way.

Howe got his team playing very good attacking football on its way up to the Premier League and kept them there for several seasons; he will be back sooner rather than later and I expect him to do well. My only question mark is whether he would have the respect of superstar players.

When thinking about this a few months ago, I singled out Frank Lampard and Steven Gerrard as mangers to watch. Since then, they have had very contrasting fortunes.

Lampard lost his job at Chelsea after a good first season in which he gave young players their chance and made light of the club's transfer ban. I think that he made the mistake of falling out with a few players and perhaps he has been shown up tactically by what Tuchel achieved when he took over. I think he needs to go to the continent and rebuild, rather than taking on a lower Premier League club. People will question whether he can handle top players – he has got to prove them wrong.

Gerrard, on the other hand, has gone from strength to strength with Rangers, reversing recent history by dominating fierce rivals Celtic and even doing well in Europe. I'm convinced that Gerrard will become manager of an elite Premier League club. Both Lampard and Gerrard have the potential to become the England manager in the future. Time will tell.

Graham Potter is another that I can see a big future for. He was quickly snapped up by Brighton after the football he produced at Swansea and he is doing well at a club that I reckon would have gone down under Chris Hughton. Expect him to go higher because his football philosophy is right for a bigger club.

Swansea must be getting fed up with losing talented managers but Steve Cooper, who has just failed to take them into the Premier League, is another good up and coming manager.

Blackpool's Neil Critchley is a name worth looking out for. He comes from good stock, having taken his first post in senior management after running Liverpool Under 23s and has had a very impressive first full season. I like the way his team plays which deservedly got The Seasiders promoted to the Championship. I was pleased that Richie Wellens has got another chance in management at my old club Donny. He may have made a mistake working for his mates at Salford, but I liked what I saw of him at Swindon.

They were calling Barrow 'the Barcelona of the National League' when they won promotion into the EFL under Ian Evatt and after watching a couple of games I could see why. Since then, he has proved himself again by turning things around at Bolton Wanderers, where he played the type of football that suggests he can manage at an elite level whilst putting another promotion on his CV. He and Ryan Lowe, of Plymouth, are my other two tips to have bright futures.

More generally, the managerial merry-go-round still churns out mediocre results. I put Sam Allardyce and David Moyes in this category. Again it's worth pointing out that they have had very different fortunes in 2021.

Big Sam is a nice guy to have a drink with, but I've never bought his reputation as a manager. Until he took on the job at West Brom last season, he made his name as someone who 'keeps clubs up'. Even that, in my view, is exaggerated as Everton, West Ham, Newcastle, Sunderland and Crystal Palace were all big enough and strong enough to warrant being in the topflight.

Apart from his short spell in charge of England, Big Sam has complained about not getting a really big job and said, if he had an Italian-sounding name, people would look at him differently. No, they wouldn't. Allardyce will never get a job with the elite clubs because of the football he plays. They look for managers who play the right way whilst Big Sam is stuck in the mould of defensive, safety first football. Getting your team organised defensively and hoping to nick something isn't good enough for the elite clubs.

I wonder if Big Sam appreciated the irony that, after doing much the same thing at The Hawthorns as Albion plunged towards relegation, they suddenly let the brakes off at Chelsea and played like a Guardiola team where they scored five goals.

Moyes did have a very good season at West Ham and looks to have changed his way of thinking. Like Big Sam, Moyes has got his reputation as a manager in an underwhelming way. I never worked out why he was regarded as such a success at Everton, one of the biggest clubs in the land. But, yes, he has produced some good attacking football in his second spell with The Hammers.

The pattern when managers who do the rounds come to a new club is nearly always the same. They immediately point out that they don't like three quarters of the players left by the previous manager and spend big money to try to put things right. In this way, clubs are often counting the cost of changing managers without necessarily moving forward.

Short term appointments usually mean that the managers do the same thing – try to get the team organised and play defensive football. Look at sides who get relegated and you'll find that nine times out of ten this is the way they play. Too often managers worry from day one about losing their job and set up their sides to keep the scoreline down rather than to win games, which is the hardest part of football.

Today's managers have a difficult time with the media who are on their backs from the start. They put them under pressure as soon as they get a couple of bad results and will say – whether true or not – that the players don't want to play for the manager.

In some ways, managers have a tougher task than in my day. The system of having a Director of Football isn't necessarily bad, providing he and the manager think the same way. But too many clubs bring in players who aren't necessarily the manager's choice. My old club, Nottingham Forest, are one example as they signed 70 players between 2017 and the start of last season.

Managers are paid to get the best out of players at their football clubs and that is harder if they are not making key decisions. In my view, this is one of the things that separates average managers from the greats. The best are those who are able to make the strong decisions, to handle players coming in and out of the club, the dressing room and the media.

Managers such as Cloughie and Sir Alex would have told owners to 'shove their clubs up their arses' if they saw interference in their decision making and I think today's great managers are the same. Klopp, Guardiola and Bielsa would all walk if they felt that they were being compromised – and that's their strength.

I love the story of Pep and how he got the Barcelona job. He speaks about when he was manager of Barcelona B and was invited out for a meal by club president, Joan Laporta. When Pep was told Laporta was thinking about promoting him to the senior role, he said that he thought he was joking and wrote down on a napkin that he didn't have the balls to give him the role.

I liked that. It was Pep's way of showing that he could handle the big occasion and he proved it by quickly telling superstars Ronaldinho, Deco and Samuel Eto'o that they weren't part of his plans.

Which brings me finally to my club Sheffield Wednesday. How we could really do with someone to make the right and tough decisions in 2021!

The best that I can say to fellow Owls fans is that we still have a hope and a dream. But I honestly think we are currently in the worst state ever in our history.

Owls fans know it's not just the fact that we have gone back down to League One. We've done that in the past and bounced back in recent seasons .It is the state of our club off the field that concerns me.

Things change very quickly and by the time that you read this we will probably know a little more about where the club is heading. My hope is that we haven't started another season with a points deduction because we all know how disastrous that proved as we went down on the final day of the 2020/21 season when needing just a single goal to pip Derby County.

As I'm writing, I don't know where we stand about the ownership of the ground which appears to have been sold off to one of Dejphon Chansiri's companies and we also have the issue of players not being paid. We are being left to guess at what is happening as Chansiri himself is not communicating with the fans which is not a good thing.

Wednesday are a big club but moving in the right direction won't be easy. Other big clubs in League One – Sunderland, Portsmouth and Ipswich – all appear to have sorted their finances out and are better placed to move forward.

In my view, when a club like Owls goes to depths like this, you must look at the decision makers and the decisions that have been made over recent years. It's obvious to me and I'm sure to many Wednesday fans that we have had too many managers and most of those appointments have been bad ones.

This leaves me to think that the only way ahead is for Chansiri to make a clean break with the club. He needs to sell and to leave us in a position where we can make a fresh start.

But we know that the club has been up for sale since 2018 and this isn't going to be easy.

Fans must wake up to owners and why they get into football. Often they see them as benefactors who invest loads of their own money in the hope of improving the club. But that runs against how these people become mega rich in the first place. Do you really think billionaires throw away their money for no reason? Usually, they offset what they are giving to a club against tax –

using money given to the football club to save a bill that one of their other companies would have had to pay.

Although they know that the club is likely to lose money unless they are in the Premier League, they are then banking on making a profit from the sale. Businessmen look for a good return on their 'investment' and Chansiri won't leave Owls unless it suits him financially.

We need the ownership to be sorted sooner, rather than later, because this time there won't be a Terry Curran to save us. What I did in coming down from the First Division to play in the Third for my club doesn't happen in 2021 and it will never happen again because the money side is now too big.

It will be interesting to see what happens to the manager, Darren Moore, and I wish him all the luck in the world. But recruiting players isn't easy when they know that the club is in a mess.

Looking on the positive side, I hope to see a full Hillsborough again and know, that whatever is happening on and off the field, our fans are some of the most loyal in the country. They have continually backed the club, both home and away, and will get behind the players given the chance and the slightest encouragement.

If this terrible last year or so has shown us anything, it is that the fans are what football is all about. We may feel used and abused but, unlike players, managers and owners, we stick with our team.

Knowing that there are 30,000 who would fill Hillsborough tomorrow is my Owls hope and dream.

Good luck to Owls and everyone in football!

Career Statistics

	Appearances	Goals
Doncaster Rovers 1973 - 1975	75	11
Nottingham Forest 1975 - 1977	60	17
Bury 1977	2	0
Derby County 1977 - 1978	29	2
Southampton 1978 - 1979	34	1
Sheffield Wednesday 1979 - 1982	138	39
Atvidaberg 1980	9	1
Sheffield United 1982 - 1983	44	3
Everton 1983 - 1985	30	1
Huddersfield Town 1985 - 1986	36	8
Panionios 1986	0	0
Hull City 1986	6	1
Sunderland 1986	9	1
Grimsby Town 1987	14	0
Chesterfield 1987	1	0
Total	**487**	**85**

Honours

Division Two Nottingham Forest	Promotion	1977
League Cup Southampton	Runners Up	1978
Division Three Sheffield Wednesday	Promotion	1980
FA Cup Everton	Winners	1984
Division One Everton	Champions	1985
FA Cup Everton	Runners Up	1985

MORGAN LAWRENCE
PUBLISHING SERVICES

**The following books are also available to purchase from
morganlawrence.co.uk and all major book retailers**

The story of Leicester City's journey from a struggling football club to one of the best teams in England, told by those who were there and were pivotal to the Club's success.

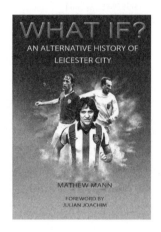

This fascinating, unique book explores some key moments in Leicester City's history and imagines what might have been.

'What If?' is a must buy for all Foxes fans.

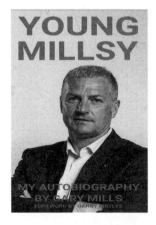

GARY MILLS took a sensational bow on the football stage becoming the youngest player to win the European Cup.

YOUNG MILLSY is a feel-good story for the half-glass-full reader who believes talent and hard work make all things possible.

**Email: hello@morganlawrence.co.uk
Telephone: 07514 116 493**